FIGHTER
RESCUER
HEALER

FIGHTER, RESCUER, HEALER –
INSPIRATION, ACTION, CHANGE

First Published in 2012 by L' Coco Publishing
Cover Art produced by Louis G Thompson
This edition © Copyright Tony Somers 2012
All images © Copyright Tony Somers 2012.

ISBN: 978 0 95726 910 1

Typeset by Ben Ottridge
benottridge.co.uk

FIGHTER
RESCUER
HEALER

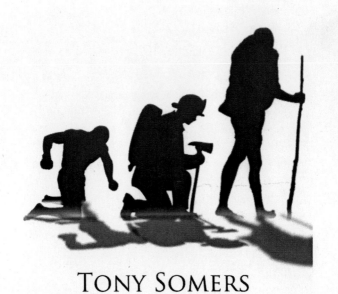

TONY SOMERS

ACKNOWLEDGEMENTS

I dedicate this book to my family. Big thanks to my mum and dad for giving me the best gift that anyone could ever have: my life.

Dad, I miss you every day and mum, you have always been a hero to me.

My brothers Paschal, Paul and John are fantastic people.

My wife Beverley, for all of her tremendous support and love.

My children, Claire and Danny, for making my life complete; I love you more than words can ever say.

All of the events in this book are true although some of the names and characters have been changed to preserve peoples confidentiality and privacy.

CONTENTS

FOREWORD
by Geoff Thompson

Let me start by saying that I have trusted the author of this beautiful book, Tony Somers, with my very life. In fact, I have trusted him with more than that; I have trusted him with my soul.

It might seem like an exaggeration, but why exaggerate when the truth is enough? My lifelong friend and I have been weaned on many decades of hard-core martial arts (the kind that either work in a combative situation or you get your own bed at the A&E) and depth psychology, where the most rigorous self-scrutiny was necessary to erase old conditioning and to re-educate (and reintegrate) debilitating shadows.

I knew Tony as a fighter; we swapped leather and scrimmaged for thousands of hours. I knew Tony when he was a firefighter; it was always his greatest ambition to escape the factory for an employ in the brigade. I trained with him in preparation for his exams and I celebrated with him when he was accepted into his dream job.

I perhaps know Tony better now as a modern-day shaman, a healer, a man who dedicates his life to the service of others. The fact that his raison d'être is service tells me that he is going to heal on a global scale.

And of course what I love most about him is the fact that he was a fighter, he was a firefighter, he has seen death, he is a man who knows pain; without that knowledge, without that colourful experience, how could he heal others?

Tony's story is an inspiration. Tony is an inspiration. I know that this book, these words, will educate, entertain and inspire anyone who is blessed enough to own a copy.

Geoff Thompson

Are we condemned to reinvent the wheels
our parents set in motion?
Are our children the sum of all the parts we play,
or something more?
The seconds drip, and pool themselves,
in many different oceans,
As we sweat ourselves to death through
every bleeding pore.

Does circumstance dictate the
growing pains of evolution?
Are free will, and consequence,
God's judgment manifest?
Anaesthetised by fear some turn
from higher expectation –
But all are cursed, and none are blessed,
If we lay our collective consciousness to rest.

Stuart Williams

INTRODUCTION

The main reason I wrote this book was to share my own experiences with you, the reader.

What I hope will come across clearly in these pages is that all through my life I have been accompanied by fear. The thing I have realised about fear is that we all experience it but no one ever talks about it.

It is very rare for someone to admit that they are scared.

I have trained with world-class martial artists, hard men and women, and they were all scared.

Tough guys on the street, business men and women, they are all scared; they won't show it but believe me, they are scared.

I have had many confrontations in and out of the ring or dojo and I was petrified every single time.

Fear is a natural emotion that comes in many guises; it can come before you give a talk or step into a new job. It can come in a close relationship when you are scared to show your feelings, perhaps fearing rejection or looking silly, or both.

This is normal – you are normal, you are not on your own. Welcome to the real world! People call fear 'the friend of exceptional people' but I feel that fear is there for all of us and we are all exceptional people.

As you will see on the pages of this book, I have always tried to face the things that scare me but they still scare me; I face them in spite of my fear.

I go to the gym to exercise; I don't go there to watch other people exercise. If I want to get fit, then I must do the work. Nobody else can do it for me.

If you want to learn how to handle your fears, then you must do the work. Fear is like the gym of life – it offers you an opportunity to train your mind. Every time you overcome a fear, no matter how big or small, you will get stronger.

One of the other things that never ceases to amaze me is how we compare ourselves to others. The worst part of this is that we normally do it in a negative way and come up short in comparison.

The ironic thing is that the person you are comparing yourself to is probably comparing himself to you, in a negative way.

To return to the gym scenario once again: I walk into the gym and see people lifting weights. I automatically assume that they are stronger than me; they have bigger muscles than me. I see someone hitting the punch bag and think: he looks sharp, fast and he hits hard, I will avoid him, he might make me look bad (he is better than me).

Even in the shower I can't help but notice (I try not to) that people are in better shape than me, they all have bigger penises than me.

You walk into a classroom for the first time and automatically assume that everyone else in that class will be more intelligent than you.

You are out on a social evening, maybe looking for a date. You see an attractive woman. Then a thought enters your head: why would she go out with me or even talk to me? There are lots of better looking and more interesting people than me in this bar.

The message that I desperately want to share with you is that the vast majority of people in the gym, in the showers, in the classroom, in the pub, in the nightclub, in life itself, feel exactly the same way as you! You are not alone, and what's more, you are a normal human being, feeling the things that normal human beings feel. I'm OK and so are you – that simple realisation will set you free.

It's a level playing field for us all; no one is any better than you. What makes the difference between people is their attitude and the subsequent choices that they make.

So choose carefully, have courage, take action and enjoy this once in a lifetime journey. You have been given a very precious gift, which is life itself!! Why not choose to make the most of it?

I am surrounded by fantastic human beings; ordinary and yet still fantastic. I can see their brilliance but for some reason they don't see what I see, they just see their ordinariness.

But why can't they see what I see? And what would happen if they did?

What stops us from seeing our brilliance? What stops us from fulfilling our potential?

The obvious answer is that we stop ourselves, but why do we do this?

Some psychologists suggest that our biggest fear is annihilation or oblivion, which many people would see as death. To protect ourselves from annihilation we cling to other people. We need other people to save us, to tell us that we are OK, to need us. Babies cling to their mothers for life; this is what we call instinct. But what if we never lose this instinct? As we grow older we change the roles of our mothers for our fathers, brothers, sisters, teachers and even friends.

We go from tribe to tribe – we have the family tribe, the work tribe, the friendship tribe, the religious tribe, and we have many other tribes to fit into and gain a sense of belonging. Our biggest fear is exclusion from these tribes, rejection by our peers and carers, because deep down we equate being rejected or excluded with death or oblivion. In history this goes back to cavemen days when the environment was so harsh and hostile that rejection would mean certain death (annihilation), but even in our personal history, as babies, when our mothers left us for the first time (even briefly), I am sure it would have felt like devastation or oblivion. Our thoughts would have been along the lines of, 'Where has she gone? And what if she never comes back?' At this stage a baby thinks it is the whole world and not just a part of it.

So, we feel as though we must fight this nauseating feeling of rejection or oblivion at all costs, and what you resist will persist. We therefore cling to the tribe for what we interpret as our survival.

We strive to be liked, to fit in, and are prepared to pay any price to do so, for the alternatives, as we have already said, are not good.

In our efforts to fit in we give up many things, not least the freedom to be whoever we want to be or were even meant to be.

We learn very early in life that we must conform and our first teachers are our parents. They have had a lifetime of conforming and are eager to pass these habits on to us, mostly, it has to be said, with good intentions.

A baby soon learns that it will not always get its needs met by crying. Its parents may leave the room for a time and it may feel as though they are never coming back.

As children we learn what behaviour is acceptable and what is not, usually by some programme of punishment and reward.

We learn how to fit in with our family tribe and then our school tribe but once again these lessons can be very harsh.

We create defence mechanisms against the fear of being rejected, we create images or personalities that we think and feel will help us to be accepted by other tribe members.

In other words, we become just like actors and we learn how to put on a show. The problem is that we forget who we really are and the role we take on becomes for all intents and purposes the real us.

Deep down you know that this is not the real you but you have played this role so convincingly and for so long that it actually now feels real.

The real you is well and truly buried below layer upon layer of tribal conditioning.

The sad thing is that you are now in a no-win situation. The expectations that have been placed upon you and which you have also placed upon yourself are too high. You can not live up to them; you start to feel like a failure. You cannot be like your dad or the superhero on the TV, or wonder woman, or the ideal mum who is always calm and never raises her voice in frustration or anger. You start to feel like a failure, a disappointment, a piece of crap.

In your quiet moments you feel a stirring, you hear a distant voice, you feel discomfort. Something or someone is pulling at your heartstrings; you feel as though something is missing, there must be more to life than this.

You start to read self-help books, spiritual texts; you feel a connection with these writings and these people and with what they are saying. You start to wonder, what if? What if the tribe were wrong? What if I have been wrong? What if I don't have to put on an act?

An internal battle rages in your mind. Talk about discomfort! This is real discomfort. The what-ifs are fighting against the past conditions – who will win?

What if I can be real? Who is the real me? What if there really is no oblivion? What if I am all there is? What if the real me, the part that I keep hidden, is OK?

Let's go on a journey of discovery together, hand in hand. I will share some of my experiences with you; however, it is important to remember that we are all teachers and pupils in the school of life.

I do not have all of the answers but I can share what I have learned so far.

I once heard a story about some scientists and a pike. The scientists decided (in their wisdom) to test the memory of the pike. They put the pike in a large tank and over a period of time they added smaller fish into the tank, which the pike dutifully and probably very happily gobbled up. Then one day they removed the pike from his tank and placed him into a holding tank. They put some smaller fish into the original tank but this time they covered them in a glass bowl, so effectively they created a tank within a tank. The pike was then placed back into the original tank. The first thing he did was dive straight at the smaller fish, at which point he smacked his snout on the glass bowl. This happened again and again over the next few weeks and eventually the pike gave up trying to get at the fish and left them alone. At this point the scientists once again removed him to the holding tank. They removed the glass bowl and allowed the smaller fish to swim freely in the larger tank. The pike was then placed back into the tank with the smaller fish. The scientists waited with baited breath. To their amazement the pike just ignored the smaller fish. He ignored them for so long that he eventually starved to death, whilst his food source happily swam right under his nose. The conclusion of this experiment was that just like Pavlov's dogs, the pike had been conditioned to believe that he could not eat the smaller fish.

It's important to realise that we have all been conditioned. From the time that we are born we are being conditioned. The biggest conditioners are our parents, who in turn were conditioned by their parents and so the conditioning goes on and on through the generations. We are conditioned by our friends, peers, media and environment. Most of this conditioning, but by no means all of it, is unfortunately negative.

A question worth asking yourself might be, what have you been conditioned to believe about yourself? What were your family values? Some of them may have been: work hard, keep your head down, be a good boy/girl. 'Big boys don't cry' can be interpreted as 'It's not good to show feelings'.

What have people told you that you can or can't do? Who do you think you are? What wonderful things are within your reach that past conditioning (just like the pike) is stopping you from reaching out and taking? Have you even realised that you have been conditioned? Because in one way or another, you definitely have.

Have you ever thought there must be more to life than this? Have you ever said to yourself, if only I had my time all over again, things would be different? If only I was younger, thinner, better looking, more intelligent, then things would be different. But who said that you are not the right size, not good looking, not intelligent? You have been told a lie and what is worse is that you have not only believed it but you have also told that same lie to yourself over and over again. I am reminded of a famous saying: 'The truth shall set you free.'

The good news is that the truth is right under your nose; you are sitting on it, but just like the pike you don't see it anymore. You are sitting on a pointed nail but it's not sharp enough yet, not painful enough yet, to sting you into action.

This is your lot so just accept it and get on with it or dare to challenge the lie, dare to reach out and bite that little fish. You have been told a lie and what makes this fact even worse is that you now keep telling that same lie to yourself, and guess what? It becomes a self-fulfilling prophecy. Who are you to write a book? Who are you to stand up and talk to people? You're not very clever, are you? Will anyone even take a second look at you?

How many times do you set yourself a fantastic goal or see a great opportunity, the chance of an amazing future? You pluck up the courage to go for it, you are so determined, excited, and then an old part of you, a fearful part of you, jumps out and, metaphorically speaking, trips you up and pulls you back into the comfort – or in many cases the discomfort – of your dreary but very well-known life.

You don't see it coming, you are not self-aware and then all of those old scenarios play out yet again and you find yourself back in that old familiar place. It's back to square one, with the same old excuses. The most popular excuse is that it's someone else's fault, never yours.

The internal voice in your mind is usually an old part of you, a part that says things like, 'Who is going to listen to you? Who do you think you are? Don't get above your station. You're working class, you're middle class, you're upper class, stay in your class. She won't want to go out with you; you're too ugly, too stupid, too old, too young, and too fat! Other people are better than you, in fact they are all better than you. Face it, you're just not good enough, you will never be a success so why even bother to try?'

These are your old fears, things that people have said to you in the past, things that you have said to yourself. They are just memories and illusions. Can you touch them? Is the person who told you that you were stupid when you were five years old still standing beside you and telling you the same thing right now? If that person is still in your adult life, then why are you still listening to them? You are the adult now, you can choose whether to listen or not. If they are not standing beside you, then why are you still listening to that old voice? At five years of age you may not have had any choice, but you do now.

I remember working with a really nice guy who came to see me because he said that he felt as though he was stuck in a rut (a rut is a coffin without the ends). He lived on his own, had few male friends, no female friends and no job. But people would tell me he was a very good guy to have around on a building site or to fix anything mechanical, such as a car or a bike.

Apparently John (not his real name) was very good at practical things; other people could see this but he couldn't. On a confidence scale of one to ten, ten being the most confident, he was at minus one in all areas of his life.

We had a few very hard counselling sessions, which normally consisted of me racking my brains to come up with some strategies to get him out of this rut. He would listen intently; from time to time his eyes would light up. However, in the next moment he would shrug his shoulders, pull a long face and say, 'Yeah, Tony, that's all well and good, BUT...' Every time I heard him say the word BUT I knew that we were going right back to the beginning again. After many frustrating attempts by myself and just as many frustrating 'buts' by him, one day he said, 'I feel as though I am stuck behind a big wall.' I was over the moon; a metaphor, fantastic! Something to work with at last, a way in. 'Let's work with that metaphor,' I enthusiastically said...

Tony: OK, John, what's this wall like?
John: Very big, solid.
Tony: Right, what tools do we need to break through this wall?
John: Oh, I can get through the wall whenever I want to.
Tony: You can? (Amazed!)
John: Oh yes, it's easy.
Tony: Then why don't you?
John: Because I know what's on this side of the

wall and I might not like what's on the other side and the not knowing is scary.

John had what I would call 'learned helplessness'. He had been brought up (conditioned) to believe that he wasn't very good at things and always needed other people to do things for him. John's parents had done everything for him throughout his whole life, from washing his clothes to fixing his bike. No doubt every time John's dad fixed the puncture on his bike he admonished John for being stupid or useless.

The message John picked up at a subconscious level as a young boy was that he was useless, a failure. The thought of doing anything on his own terrified him. After all, how could someone who considered or believed himself to be a useless failure survive on his own? Who would want to know him? How could anyone ever like somebody like him?

The ironic thing is that John hated being on his side of the wall as it was getting too uncomfortable for him and he was starting to get inquisitive about what was waiting for him on the other side. As far as I know, he is still stuck on his side of the wall; his own fears and past conditioning are keeping him a prisoner there. The wall is in his own head and has been put there over the years by himself and many other significant people in his life. The wall is meant to keep him safe, to save him from oblivion, to keep his fears at bay, to keep them out, but actually all they do is keep him trapped in a world full of frustration, misery and fear. But at least he is alive, and to step out from his world of learned helplessness would be to risk failure, hurt, rejection and to confirm his belief that he is useless, which could in turn lead to our old friend, annihilation.

Some people might say any attention, even bad attention, is a good thing. Any love, even bad love, is a good thing; it's better than NOTHING! Or should I say *being* NOTHING!

I have learned in no uncertain terms that fear is the enemy of a happy life and as such must be faced. Fear and ignorance are the things that stop us from questioning our conditioning and beliefs and in doing so they stop us from growing towards our full potential. Fear's biggest accomplice is denial. The enemy of fear is love, and love's biggest accomplice is courage. Having courage does not mean that you never experience fear; it means that you can face the fear or even learn to live with it.

WHAT IS FEAR?

Before we look at what fear is we need to know how our minds work. I am going to keep this very simple. This is a very complex area and even those people who are experts in this field are changing their own minds and constantly coming up with new theories. The theory I am going to talk about is something that I have discovered through painstaking and very personal research.

The important thing to remember is that we create our own world or at least our own version of it. Our brains consist of millions upon millions of neurons and chemicals. These neurons communicate with each other by passing electrical charges via their individual transmitters. We are actually born with far more neurons than we ever need. Imagine a children's play pen – the type that are full of lots of brightly coloured balls and the kids have great fun diving right into the middle of them, disappearing from sight and then, when they get bored, seeing how far they can throw them. Well, metaphorically speaking, our brains are like those play pens – the neurons are the brightly coloured balls.

In Susan A. Greenfield's book, *The Private Life of The Brain*, she writes, 'The degree of meaning that we covertly apportion to each person, object, and event as we blunder around in the outside world will, in turn, be matched by a corresponding degree of neurone connections.'

So every time something happens in our lives, and this can be anything, new pathways are formed by the neurons, or brightly coloured balls, joining together. Once these pathways have been formed the theory is that they can never be erased.

The good news, however, is that there are enough neurons still left to form new and even stronger pathways. A simple example of this is a small child gets frightened by a dog; a pathway is formed inside his mind. The pathway is a newly formed belief that all dogs are dangerous. This pathway will stay in place and each time he sees a dog, new neurons will be added to the pathway, making it stronger and stronger and his fear and dislike of dogs will grow. To get over this newly formed fear of dogs, he would need to have a positive experience with a dog and this would have to be continually reinforced, creating a new and even stronger pathway which would let him know that not all dogs are dangerous.

This whole process is happening every second that we are alive and no two people are ever the same as we all form unique pathways. So you can now see why I say we create our own minds. Knowing this allows us to concentrate on forming new pathways that we want and need. We can basically create or form our own map of the world, and how exciting is that thought? Some people even believe that we create our own worlds.

It's worth remembering that your perception is your reality. In other words, the way that you see the world makes that version of the world real for you.

If you see the world through rose-tinted spectacles, then the world will be rose-tinted.

If you see the world through dark lenses, then the world will be dark.

However, what is real for you may not be real for me and vice versa – remember that we all wear different lenses.

This is why we all respond differently to different situations. Some people are constantly negative, they have negative influences and so have negative pathways, whereas some people have positive influences and so create positive pathways. This theory applies to emotions like fear, anger, love and happiness, and can also be applied to people with addictions; in other words, they have addictive pathways which they continually reinforce.

This is well worth keeping in mind as you will see throughout this book that I am a big believer in facing my fears. At a neurological level you will see that I am constantly forming new and stronger pathways towards a happier and freer life. I hope that after reading this book you will realise that you can choose to do the same and change your life forever.

Whether you like it or not, you are forming new neurological pathways every day but with this knowledge you can choose to create the pathways that you want, instead of other people or life in general forming your pathways for you and so dictating how you will live your life. You can choose, so why not start choosing now how you want to live your life?

The dictionary definition of fear (there are many) suggests that fear is a painful emotion that can be shown or hidden and is connected to a painful event or a perceived threat.

Deepak Chopra suggests fear is a jolt from the past: it reminds us of the moment when we left a place of belonging and found ourselves in a place of vulnerability. The Bhagavadgita suggests that fear is born of separation, implying that the original cause of fear was the loss of unity. Ultimately, that separation is not a fall from grace but a loss of who you really are. This loss of who you really are or the place of vulnerability are other words for oblivion or death.

Think about this: if at a subconscious level you feel vulnerable or you do not know who you really are, then surely the fear of death or oblivion will not be far away. One of the ways I cope with fear in my life is to remind myself of who I am and why I am here.

One of my earliest memories as a small child was of having an overwhelming sense of love for my parents. Then one day, and I can't remember how these thoughts came into my mind, I started to think of what would happen if they should die. How would I feel? I sat alone in my bedroom and cried at the thought of them not being there. They were perfectly healthy as far as I knew but there I was sitting on the end of my bed and crying my heart out. Was I crying for them or myself? If they died, I would be alone, abandoned, rejected. Who would look after me? Who, more importantly, would love me? They were my carers, my mentors, my heroes, they knew everything, they kept me safe, they were my giants in a world that to a small boy seemed as though it was overflowing with giants. The thought of them not being there, of being separated from them in any way let alone by something as tragic as death, was terrifying.

At that time in my life they defined who I was. I was Anthony, their oldest son, they loved me and that's all I needed to know. Without them, who would I be? I learned at an early age that all fear is based around abandonment and rejection, which can also come from a loss of face or identity. We create a picture or an image of who we are and how we would like other people to see us and if that image gets threatened our levels of fear go into overdrive.

I have a friend who is a really nice guy; he works very hard on his people skills and is well liked by most people. However, as I got to know him a little bit better I could see a darker side to his personality. This darker side would emerge if anyone threatened his nice guy image. He would change from Mr Nice to Mr Nasty in an instant. He was actually very aggressive and very intimidating; in fact, he was as far away from Mr Nice as you could get. He had worked very hard at putting this image of a nice but tough guy out into the world. It was how he saw himself and how he wanted everyone else to see him.

My guess is that deep down he was full of insecurities, as most of us are. Rather than face these insecurities he would attack anyone who threatened the exterior version of himself that he had painstakingly created.

If I am not who I think I am, then who am I? If I have this image of myself and you don't like me, then you might reject me or abandon me and then where will I be? How would it feel to be abandoned or rejected? We are back to that little boy again, crying on the end of his bed with the terrifying thought of being abandoned and left all alone. When we lose people, do we cry for them or for ourselves?

However we define it, the one thing you can be certain of is that fear is natural and thankfully is here to stay. Let me just repeat that: fear is natural. If you experience fear, it doesn't mean that you are weak, weird or not a real man or woman. In fact, it's just the opposite – you are a real person feeling real emotions. You are a human being and that entails many emotions.

Fear and death are both very natural but also very rarely talked about subjects in our society. To show fear is taken as a sign of weakness and nobody wants to admit that one day they are going to die. We all know it but we don't want to face it. We see it happen to other people but secretly think our own demise is still a long way off. At this point I am reminded of an old song with the words 'enjoy yourself, it's later than you think'. Another good point to remember is that none of us will get out of this life alive!

Look at any disaster in the world, watch it unfold on TV, watch the terror on people's faces. I guarantee you that when a government spokesman or some such person stands up to talk about the disaster you have just watched with your own eyes, you won't hear them mention fear. Oh no, that would never do – the people involved were brave, courageous, but never scared. Where did the fear go? It was definitely there, we all saw it.

Fear is an emotion which is often denied, not just by individuals but by whole countries. George Bush looked like a very frightened man during the events of 9/11. But did he ever mention fear or being scared? If he did, I didn't hear it but I did hear him ranting on about revenge and hitting back. Could this have been out of fear? The rest is history. As we have all witnessed, fear begets fear and it can spread through whole countries and indeed continents. Imagine how the world would look now if George Bush had said, 'Let's forgive them, let's not drop down to their level. We are better than that.' I guess he would have got shot by some other fearful American but maybe the world would be a better place and what an example for arguably the most powerful man in the world to set.

We all know fear is there, we all feel it; just because we deny it doesn't mean that it will go away. I would say it's just the opposite; the fact that we do deny it only gives it mystical power over us and makes it seem even stronger. Remember, what we resist will persist. If we accepted fear, if we dived into it, if we picked it apart, most of it would evaporate into thin air.

So if fear is so painful, why does it exist at all? Without fear, the human species would not be around today; fear has kept us alive. Our caveman ancestors would certainly have needed fear to survive. Imagine them going up to a sabre-toothed tiger and saying, 'Aarr, what a cute little pussy cat.' We learn what to be afraid of and to act accordingly, usually with pure adrenalin-driven fear. Even today we are born into a world with many dangers and fear is a vital emotion if we are to survive. Fear makes us look for that first contact with our mothers once the umbilical cord is cut.

Fear can be a motivator in many different ways; for example, I have worked with many university students who get a huge rush of fear when they realise that they are about to fail their degrees after three years of study unless they hand their dissertations in before a looming deadline. In this case, it is the fear of failure that motivates them to get a move on and it often works!

For the purpose of this book I am going to break fear down into two areas. Firstly, fear that we need, that's the fear we have said is vital for survival. This is the type that will keep you alive, the type people call gut instinct, your early warning system. I remember as a kid there was a wall I could never climb over, although most of my friends could. The fact that I couldn't climb the wall caused me to be the brunt of many a joke – 'Anthony is a girl, Anthony is a girl, can't climb the wall, scared he's gonna fall.' I always had a bit of a fear of heights so I wasn't too bothered about climbing it anyway and I would subtly disappear whenever climbing it was on that day's agenda.

Then one day while we were playing football in our little close a very vicious Alsatian dog called Rebel, that had attacked a few people in his time, usually postmen or women, decided just out of the blue, maybe he was bored or something (you know how some dogs are), to home in on me. I saw him out of the corner of my eye as he started to descend the stairs of the maisonette where he and his useless owners lived. We all stopped dead in our tracks. I think Frank Jones, who was the biggest cheat at sports I have ever met, used this opportunity to score a goal and even though we told him it wouldn't count he was running around screaming as if he had scored the winning goal in a Wembley cup final.

We all waited with baited breath, frozen to the spot. Who was he after? He bounded straight towards me. Even though I was clearly his target, no one was taking any chances. They all scampered off in different directions; after all, he was entitled to change his mind if he felt like it – he was massive. We used to joke, 'Where does Rebel sleep at night in that small maisonette?', to which someone (usually Frank) would reply, 'Wherever he fucking wants to.'

To say I shit myself would be the understatement of the year. My fear of Rebel was much greater than my fear of heights. I would have run through that wall let alone over it. Quicker than you could say 'mad fucking dog alert', for the first time ever I was on the other side of that wall. Fear can be and very often is a great motivator.

I believe fear saved me that day and has many times since. It wasn't until I sat down to write this book that I remembered Rebel. I hated that dog. The ironic thing is I am now the proud owner of a beautiful Alsatian whose original name, believe it or not, was Rebel (I quickly changed his name to Duke). I had created a strong and negative neurological pathway around Alsatians but by owning Duke I have created a new and positive pathway towards Alsatians. He is a great dog, loyal, faithful and a good companion and very soft natured.

This is the type of fear that we definitely do not want to lose but like all our emotions we need to control it. A very high percentage of doctors now believe that up to 80 % of all illnesses are caused by stress. If you think about this statement, what they are actually saying is that a large percentage of all illnesses are caused in the mind. It is my belief that emotions like fear, anger and guilt play a big part in this.

Fear is a great emotion, a real necessity for survival, but you must learn how to control it. Mike Tyson's trainer said fear is like fire; if you control it, it can give you warmth, you can cook on it and it gives light, but let it get out of control and it can kill you. Those doctors may just know what they are talking about after all.

When we are scared our bodies will go into survival mode, which basically means they prepare themselves for fight or flight. The problem with this whole process is that in the body's efforts to prepare for fight or flight the brain closes down the functions that we don't need in the heat of the moment. For example, our sexual system – most stressed people don't have good sex lives. I don't know about you but if a tiger was chasing me I don't think I would be thinking about having sex! Our growth systems close down; the body is not thinking about growth, just surviving. Most importantly of all, your body will close down its immune system while in fight or flight mode. So remember, when you are stressed, scared or angry you are leaving your body open to attack from all sorts of illness, the protective barriers are down. The next time you are stressed think about this process and then ask yourself, is the problem you are faced with worth making yourself ill over? Because that is what might happen.

The second type of fear (and this is the one I really want to concentrate on in this book) is the fear we create in our own minds using those brightly coloured balls again and neurological pathways. This type of fear does not help us, although I am sure it thinks it does.

Imagine you are on an aeroplane and the pilot announces that the plane is in trouble. He is going to have to crash land in the sea. I am guessing that everyone on that plane would experience a significant degree of fear, and rightly so. The pilot lands the plane on the sea and everyone is asked to make their way in an orderly fashion to the exits. Everybody is wearing their bright yellow life jackets and are specifically told not to inflate them until they have left the aircraft. However, people start to panic and inflate the jackets, making themselves twice as big, twice as hard to get past and making it twice as difficult to get off the plane. What was an orderly evacuation is now chaos – there is a strong chance that some people will not get off the plane and will be drowned.

In this example, the first fear on hearing that the plane is going to make a crash landing is justified, whereas the second wave of fear in which people start to inflate their life jackets is not justified and causes the very thing that they were afraid of happening (death) to happen anyway. This is what is happening in our lives all of the time. We put on the life jacket of fear, then inflate it and make life so much harder for ourselves and often bring about our own downfall, which could have been easily avoided with just a little bit of patience and courage.

Over the next few chapters in this book I am going to talk about the one area that I do consider myself to be an expert in, and that is indeed myself. I would also consider you to be an expert in yourself. You have got to be, you know yourself better than anyone else in the whole wide world. Doctors, life coaches, psychiatrists will all tell you that they are the experts on you. They may be experts and as such they have much to offer but you are the expert when it comes to you. I hope that by sharing my experiences with you and explaining my own fears and insecurities, some of which I have conquered and some of which are still waiting to be faced, you will feel empowered to take on your own fears, the ones that are holding you back, and deflate them forever. One thing is certain; you are not alone in your fears and self-doubts. I have never met a single other human being, no matter how successful they may appear to be, who is not racked with fear and insecurity.

Fear comes in many disguises; I can remember on a regular basis excitedly waiting for my wife to come home from work. I hadn't seen her all day, she didn't finish work until ten o'clock in the evening and I really missed her. I would listen for her key turning in the door, at which point my heart would race but then as she walked into the room, I would deliberately try to play it cool, not even averting my gaze away from the TV. I would just utter a cold hello. On the inside I wanted to jump up, hug her and kiss her but my fear of showing my feelings meant that they stayed hidden. Remember, big boys don't cry (or show feelings).

The ironic thing is that to have shown my feelings to her would have been fine and would have even strengthened our relationship.

I have split the chapters on my life into three areas: the fighter, the rescuer and the healer; I hope you enjoy the book.

THE FIGHTER

I have called this section the fighter. The first thing I want to say about fighters is that they get scared, they feel fear...

When I look back over my life I realise that fear has always been a close companion of mine, especially in two ways: a fear of confrontation, and a fear of not being good enough. Knowing what I know now I can trace these fears back to a fear of rejection, which feeds into the fear of oblivion. If I get into a confrontation, I may lose and then I will feel like a failure and people will reject me. If I get into a confrontation with you, then you may not like me and you may reject me. If you reject me, then it will confirm my deep-seated belief that I am not good enough and if you don't believe that I am good enough, and I don't even believe that I am good enough, then what hope is there for me?

I actually end up rejecting myself and without even meaning to you just confirm my feelings of low self-worth.

If you don't think I am good enough in any area, then you may reject me. This is a vicious circle and one that can be very hard to break.

On the positive side, it is also my own personal belief that I am guided. My mum used to tell me as a small boy that everyone has a guardian angel.

She also told me about Father Christmas and the bogeyman, both of whom I have stopped believing in long ago. However, I still choose to believe in my guardian angel and whoever he or she is has had to work very hard on my behalf.

There have been times in my life when I have felt that my guardian angel has gone AWOL and I have been very alone but he or she always came back and never really went away in the first place.

I do not class myself as a religious person but I do believe in God. My God is a creator; he loves me and only wants the best for me, and of course you. He has made me and you into creators; I create my life and so do you.

I do not believe in a God of hellfire and damnation but one of love, forgiveness and compassion. Babies won't go to hell or purgatory if they are not christened (I was told this). You will not go to hell for masturbating or being gay. Women are not second-class citizens who should be heard and not seen and walk ten feet behind their husbands.

When I was about five years old, I overheard my Auntie Mag from Dublin telling my mum, after I had walked her to church, 'There is something very special about Anthony.' She is long dead but I have never forgotten those words.

Plenty of other people throughout my life have called me other things as far away from special as you can get. But her words have always stayed with me. Words are incredibly powerful seeds. I hope that my Auntie Mag is my guardian angel because she had a major impact on my life with those words.

Whoever came up with the saying 'Sticks and stones may break my bones but words will never hurt me', must have been an idiot. Wars have been started over words, the divorce courts are full because of words, and they do hurt!

I have always had an interest in sports, especially boxing, the Ali and Frazier era being a particular favourite of mine. I remember my dad and his brother, my Uncle Austin, taking me to the local boxing club as a young child. They knew the trainer from what they classed as the good old days back in Dublin. To be honest, I can't remember if I wanted to go or not, all I know is that I did go. I was put straight into the ring to see what I was made of; in those days it was a case of sink or swim.

I was shaking like a leaf; the place stank of sweat, there were bloodstains on the floor and that didn't bode well for me. I boxed one round and didn't have a clue what I was doing. I guess I tried to look like my hero Ali but I felt more like Norman Wisdom or Lee Evans, punching thin air and tripping over my own feet. I was in more danger of causing myself an injury than of ever being hurt by my opponent. It must have been hilarious to watch, just like a scene from an old Laurel and Hardy movie where poor Laurel runs around in circles with his shorts pulled up above his head so that his opponent can't hit him (in boxing you are not allowed to hit below the belt line).

I can't remember too much about the sparring that day, I think I just clung on to my opponent for dear life in the hope that he wouldn't hit me and I wouldn't have to hit him. My fear was that if I punched him, then he would punch me back, and I certainly didn't like the thought of that.

At the end of the round the trainer, who was a nice guy, came up to me and said, 'You did well there, son, you took a good thump on the nose but you kept going.' At which point I burst into tears. My dad and uncle were not best pleased and dragged me out of there as quickly as they could. I was terrified but I was trying very hard not to show my fear – even at that age I had learned to hide my feelings. When the trainer put his arms around me and showed me some compassion, I took this as permission to show my real feelings, hence my uncontrollable tears.

I was too young to care (or so I thought) and soon got over it but I think dad's pride was seriously dented. The shame of it – his oldest son crying like a big baby and in front of everyone at the Bell Green club (he drank there as well). Dad was one of those people who believed you learned most from life in the hard school of knocks.

I remember one day walking in front of a swing and taking the full force of the swing and the person sitting on it straight in the side of my head. As I lay prostrate on the ground people rushed to see if I was OK. I wasn't knocked out but might as well have been – the world was spinning and I didn't know where I was. My dad just walked off and said, 'You won't do that again in a hurry, will you?' The same thing happened when I was bitten by a dog, and when I was twelve and someone smashed a chair leg over my head during an argument (let me tell you, that hurt). All my dad said to me after I got back to my feet was, 'You went down like a big baby.' All of these events were reinforcing my belief that I couldn't live up to my dad's expectations of me and that as a son I was a big disappointment to him. He had never actually said this but it was how I internalised his actions, or in my eyes, his lack of actions/feelings towards me. Feelings of failure and shame abounded in my young and very impressionable mind.

From what I could gather his dad was a lot tougher on him but I knew deep down that he loved me in his own way. He just didn't do feelings and couldn't show it. The only time I hugged him was when I got to the hospital a few minutes after he had died. I knew he couldn't stop me and I had always wanted to do it, so I did. It broke my heart to see my dad in the last few days of his life in a hospital bed. He was a proud man. I never saw him cry but one day in the hospital, when all his strength was nearly gone, I watched him lift himself up off his bed. This might not sound like a big thing to do but I could tell it took all of the remaining strength in his body. I moved towards him to help him but he refused my offer, gritted his teeth and forced his tired and fragile body to move. I saw tears in his eyes and a look of bewilderment and anguish spread across his face, as if to say, 'How the hell did it get to this?'.

I sat there with tear-filled eyes, not saying a word but thinking, you beautiful, stubborn old bastard. I hope he is looking down and reading this now, this bit is just for him: I love you dad and I hope you are as proud of me as I am of you, and by the way, I am writing this with tear-filled eyes and an aching heart. I miss you.

I digress. Going back in time again, I also remember the Bruce Lee era when everywhere you went, especially at school, people were coming at you with flying kicks and making weird screeching noises. You would be walking down the long, grey corridors thinking about or dreading the next maths lesson, then suddenly John O'Malley would jump out of nowhere and throw a spinning roundhouse kick at your head. He always tended to miss but then he would stand there in a Bruce-Lee-like pose, staring aggressively at you through his NHS steel-rimmed spectacles, which were by now precariously perched on the end of his big nose, whilst at the same time making really funny breathing noises and gearing himself up to launch another deadly attack at any second. Although this was his nastiest, most vicious pose, I just knew that there was no menace behind it, no bad intent. It took my best efforts not to laugh out loud – I knew John was trying really hard to be scary, so just to be kind I didn't laugh. Then he would say, 'Oh all right, Anthony, are you on the way to maths class?' We would walk to the maths class as if nothing had happened. I know this sounds like really weird behaviour but it was so common place back then that it was accepted as the norm. The days just wouldn't have been the same if you weren't being attacked by a mini

Bruce Lee clone at least a dozen times before the home-time bell.

At that time David Carradine was on the TV starring as a monk called Kwai Chang Caine in *Kung Fu*. I loved that programme – he was so gentle, and yet if forced to be (and some idiot or fool normally made the mistake of forcing him), he could be physically devastating. The good guy, after much unnecessary provocation, always won through in the end. I went along to a Kung Fu club; these were shooting up everywhere and I saw myself as the next Caine. I was very easily bored in those days and tried lots of things; as well as kung fu there was karate, judo and even boxing again, but I never stuck at any of them for very long. This lack of commitment, which was often picked up on by my mum ('You never stick at anything!') yet again reinforced my internalised belief about being a failure and not being good enough.

I think sometimes life is about planting seeds and going to the various martial arts and boxing clubs were seeds that were to come back to me in a big way later in my life.

I realised very early in life that if I wanted to please people and I wanted respect I was going to have to be tough. I have since learned that every human being wants to feel significant, respected, valued and loved. They might not tell you that they want to feel these things but deep down it is what we all want. This fact is well worth bearing in mind whenever you talk to another person; they want what you want and that is to feel special. I have learned that if you can make a person feel special then you will have a friend for life. This is not hard to do; the simplest way of making someone feel significant or special is just to listen to them. Let me repeat that: just listen to them. Sounds simple, doesn't it? But it is far from simple – try it, give it a go. People from the darker sides of our society know this information and use it to their advantage. For example, paedophiles do this to their victims; they listen to them and groom them, all the time telling them that they are special and making them feel special.

If we were all raised to believe that we are special, which I believe we all are anyway, then there would be far fewer problems in the world and far fewer insecure people.

We all have our own ways of getting that feeling of significance; some people act tough, and some people act soft. Some people even make themselves ill so that people will care for them.

I was the eldest of four brothers who lived on a large council estate which was known locally as Dodge City. To be fair, I loved my life there – it was like one great big adventure playground.

It was all I knew and I believe that the human species will adapt to almost any surroundings. I felt from an early age in Dodge City that to get that feeling of significance or respect in this environment I was going to have to be tough. The problem with wanting to be tough was that it just wasn't me; I was a very gentle child who cried easily and didn't like confrontation. In hindsight that's probably why my dad wanted me to box but at the time I was having none of it. I didn't want to get punched in the face and I didn't want to punch anyone else either.

My mum's attempts to toughen me up consisted of sending me back out to face my attackers whenever I came home crying after being hit. She would go mad and say, 'Don't come home here crying to me. Get back out there and hit them back and don't come back until you do.' She would also add on 'and be careful'. How about that for a mixed message? Go out there and hit them back but be careful. I don't know about your world, but in my world hitting someone back and being careful just don't go together. This just made me feel even worse. How could I go and hit the person who had just hit me? Wouldn't they just hit me again, and what's more, even harder this time? I used to have to lie to my mum (sorry mum) and tell her, 'I did it, mum, I hit him back, he won't do that again in a hurry, I can tell you.' I felt that the expectations of my mum were that as a boy and the oldest son I should be tough. But

I wasn't and once again I felt as though I was a disappointment and a failure, a nobody.

My mum had a very tough upbringing in Dublin, with both of her parents dying when she was very young. She had to be tough but she also had a big heart. She could be very hard but she was also generous to a fault and although she never said the words 'I love you', I never doubted that she did love me. For example, if we wanted to go on school trips she would take on extra cleaning work to pay for them (money was very tight). She not only looked after four boys and ran a house, she also went out to work. She did not have an easy life and to this day she is still one of my heroes.

Me having this gentle and soft nature wasn't really a big help towards surviving on the streets of Dodge City, although I couldn't honestly say that I was horrendously bullied or regularly beaten up. It did happen but not that often and not continuously. I think that this was probably down in a lot of ways to a family called the Jones. They were a big Irish family of eight boys whose parents were big pals with my mum and dad. Most of them were older than me and although they were really lovely people, they were pretty tough and nobody tried to bully them; well, not if they had any sense. The fact that I was friends with them was enough to scare all but the hardened bullies away. 'You touch me and I will

get Dave Jones on to you,' was my favourite get-
out-of-jail-free card.

It was while I was with Dave that an incident
took place that had a big effect on my life (I got
into quite a few incidents with Dave, Frank and
Martin Jones). In the scale of things this incident
was nothing special but it brought home to me
yet again that being tough was a way to get
respect. We were walking through our council
estate, which was quite big, and wandered into a
part where I wouldn't normally go. People used
to joke that this neck of the woods was twinned
with Beirut (I am not trying to insult anyone
from Beirut). I had just started junior school and
could see some of my new school friends in the
distance. It was the first time I had seen any of
them outside school and I was really excited.
'Hey look, Dave, there are Johnny, Jim, Alex and
Fred.' Dave wasn't impressed, he was a type of
Clint Eastwood character; calm, cool with an air
of toughness around him. 'So what,' he replied.
As we approached them I couldn't wait to say
hello and thought that they would be so pleased
to see me.

We walked straight through the middle of them.
I had a great big cheesy smile on my face; after
all, these were my new school mates, they would
all know of Dave and here I was walking side by
side with him. I was as proud as punch and said
hello to every one of them by their first name and

not one of them acknowledged me but they all bowed down to Dave.

'Yes, Your Majesty, can I kiss your arse, Your Majesty, who is that little nobody beside you, Your Majesty?' I am exaggerating here but in reality Dave didn't care one little bit. I think he just gave one cool nod of his head which covered his reply to all of them in one go.

I felt proud to be with Dave and he was always a great friend to me but yet again I realised that being considered soft would get me a completely different reaction to being considered hard.

Although I didn't realise it at the time, this incident really hurt as I wanted to belong and fit in with my new school friends but instead I felt completely rejected by them. Even at this early age my belief about not being good enough was growing and this type of event just reinforced that belief.

It took quite a few years but things started to change for me when I went to Cardinal Wiseman Secondary School for Boys. I was twelve years old. In those days, there was no guided tour around the school. Frank Jones and I, who were starting secondary school together, were just told to follow Dave. After all, he knew the way; he was in the second year of the school and was given the task of keeping an eye on us. Now

Frank Jones was a completely different character to Dave. While Dave was cool, a man of few words, Frank was loud and didn't know when to shut up. Frank could start a fight in an empty house and often got me into scrapes as a kid.

A typical trick of Frank's was to shout an insult at a passer-by, or break a window just to get a chase. We would be casually walking through Wood End when crash, Frank would throw a brick through a window for no apparent reason and shout 'Run!'.

One day he had the great idea of giving all the dogs in Wood End (there were a lot of them) chocolate laxatives. At the time we thought it was hilarious as the dogs lapped up the laxatives and we pictured their owners' faces later in the day as the dogs let rip. Being a dog owner now this doesn't sound so funny but to a young kid it was great fun.

The first time I saw Wiseman's I was petrified. It was massive compared to St Patrick's junior school. Wiseman's was a sprawling mass of grey, drab concrete classrooms. The whole place had a foreboding look and feel to it. On the first day at the first break time I caught up with Frank; we had been placed in different classes. It felt unfortunate at the time but in hindsight being split up from Frank was definitely a good thing. I hate to think of the consequences for me if we had been placed in the same class. Frank was trouble with a capital 'T'. We sat on some steps that led down to the playground and both agreed that after only three hours at our new school we hated it. It was too big, had too many kids, the teachers were bullies and we were scared.

Just then we were approached by a ginger-haired lad from the year above. He obviously noticed our discomfort and in his own sensitive way decided to try to make us feel better. He said, 'You two look nervous.' We said nothing. 'It will get a lot worse, you know. Soon you will get your heads shoved down the toilet and then you will get the shit kicked out of you.' I wanted to cry but kept telling myself, don't cry you are at the big school now and big boys don't cry. Ginger was loving our obvious discomfort and was about to say something else when Dave Jones popped up. 'Is this ginger twat–' a very apt name under the circumstances '–giving you any trouble, lads?' I wanted to say no; I didn't want to upset the ginger twat as he might come after me later. But Frank being Frank jumped up. 'Yes, Dave, he is, he said he was going to shove our heads down the toilet and kick the shit out of us.' He hadn't exactly said that he was going to do this, only that at some point someone would do it. I wanted to tell Dave this but knew it was too late. My stomach turned as Dave said, 'Oh, is that right, you ginger twat?' Bang! Dave let Ginger have it, but to his credit he gave as good as he got. They stood there toe to toe, trading non-stop kicks and punches, as a big crowd gathered shouting, 'Fight! Fight! Fight' I sneaked off and melted into the crowd, shaking like a leaf.

A few days later school life was starting to settle down. Cardinal Wiseman's was one of the few schools in Coventry with a swimming pool, and what's more, we were allowed to use it after school for free. I asked Frank if he fancied a swim one night after school and we made arrangements to meet up the following evening.

I met Frank at the entrance to the swimming pool, which was locked. We were told by a passing teacher that the caretaker would be there soon to open up. Frank and I sat down by the door and waited, passing the time with idle chat about our early school experiences. We didn't notice three older boys approaching us from behind until they were right on top of us. The ringleader, a boy I later found out to be called Paddy Murphy, who had a permanent scowl on his face, hissed, 'What do you two want?'

'We are just waiting for the pool to open,' I replied. I didn't like the look of him but felt OK as we had done nothing wrong – why would he want to bother us? He turned to Frank and said, 'Have you got any brothers at this school?' Frank reeled off the names of his brothers who were still at the school and just for good measure told him the names of the ones who had left as well. He turned to me. 'What about you, have you got any older brothers here?' I replied 'no' and just as quickly as the word left my mouth his shoe filled it. I was still sitting down as he showered me with punches and kicks. I could feel the venom and pure anger in his blows, his whole demeanour said hate, anger, shit, fuck you and fuck the whole world. I was a lowlife nothing to him. I guess, knowing what I now know, that this was how he really saw himself. He was transferring all the shit in his life on to me via his fists and boots. Frank screamed, 'Leave him alone or my brothers will kill ya!' Hearing this he stopped, scowled at Frank and walked away.

I could taste my own blood but I wasn't badly hurt. I had covered up well and took most of the blows on my head and hands. But this time I couldn't hold back the tears. I was hurt more emotionally than physically. Why had he hit me? What had I done wrong? Once again I felt rejected. Why, unless there was something wrong with me, would a perfect stranger beat me up? It must have been my fault. I felt useless. Once again I had disappointed everybody; my friends, my family and myself. I was indeed a failure, worthless, a piece of crap.

Anger, as it often does, replaced my hurt. We walked home in silence but on the inside I was raging. What would I do when my brothers came to this school and met a bully like the one who had laid into me? Would I just stand there and cry? No way. I loved my brothers and had always been brought up with the message blood is thicker than water: 'You always stick up for your brothers, you're the oldest.' I made a decision right there and then. This would be the last time that I would ever let anyone hit me without fighting back. My mum was right; I would gain people's respect by fighting for it. No bullying piece of shit like the guy outside the swimming baths would ever hit me again without paying a heavy price for it. No more mister nice guy – it was time to bury the old gentle me and be reborn as a much harder person. I was at the wall of fear again; my fear of Rebel had once helped me to get over my fear of heights. This horrible feeling of shame, hurt and worthlessness would help me to overcome my fear of confrontation, although little did I know that this would be a very long road and much bigger walls were waiting to be climbed.

Over the next year I had thirteen fights, most of them just little scuffles, but this was a big turnaround for me. I even took on the school bully, who was a vicious boy who had moved to Coventry from London. Everyone was terrified of him. Some parents took their children out of the school because he made their lives so miserable. One day I was play-fighting with a boy from my class and this bully came up behind me, spun me around and pinned me up against the wall by my throat. I was so terrified, I couldn't even talk. The fact that he was squeezing my windpipe didn't help either. He told me that if he ever saw me messing around again he would batter me. He let me go and I did nothing. Everyone looked at me. By now I had gained a reputation for being a bit of a fighter but this guy was scary. He was big for our age, had a skinhead haircut and a permanent look etched on his face that said, 'Do not fuck with me.'

I walked away, my head bowed down in shame. Once again those feelings of disappointment, failure and that feeling of being a piece of crap flooded my entire body and I did not like it. I was really angry with myself and remembered the swimming pool incident; I had vowed that no one would ever pick on me again without me at least fighting back. I had broken my vow; I was disgusted with myself, I felt that dreaded feeling of shame start to enfold my body and mind. Maybe I wasn't meant to fight back; maybe this was just how life was meant to be. It felt as though every time my life was going well and I was having fun, someone would come along and bring me crashing back down into harsh reality.

I knew this bully would come again and I didn't have to wait long – the following week the bully swaggered up to me again, obviously expecting to intimidate me like he had done previously. As soon as he opened his bullying mouth I punched him and kept on punching him, years of not fighting back, of crying like a baby, of being told to get back out there and fight, of guilt and shame, of not being good enough, came spewing out with the force of a hurricane. He fought back but by taking the initiative I had gained the upper hand. Two teachers pulled us apart; unfortunately for me a male teacher gripped me and held on tightly, while a female teacher tried in vain to restrain him. He was very aggressive and pushed her out of the way. I just saw him at the last second as he launched a flying headbutt at my face. I instinctively put my head down and his head hit mine. It bloody hurt me but it must have hurt him as well. I had a lump the size of a large egg on my forehead. The teachers all knew what he was like and carted him away, and after a telling off they let me go – I was never a troublemaker.

I walked into my classroom and the whole place just erupted. People were clapping, cheering and banging desk lids. Even the teacher was smiling as she told everyone to sit down. They all really feared and hated the bully and were just relieved that someone had at long last stood up to him. It was hard to believe that a couple of months before I had been a crying wreck at the feet of another bully. Now I was a hero and it was a much nicer feeling than being a victim. I felt accepted, wanted, significant. I was OK – people liked me.

My peers and friends were not only accepting me but cheering for me as well. A few more people challenged the bully after my escapade; the belief that he was an unbeatable monster was gone and he left the school a few weeks after our fight.

Beliefs are so powerful. Once the belief that this bully was unbeatable had been smashed, other people were ready to stand up to him.

I was always scared of confrontation but even more scared of that horrible feeling of just lying there crying after being beaten up. I had buried the gentle little Anthony but I knew very well that he was still in there somewhere. My name was mentioned whenever boys got together to talk about who was the toughest in the school year, which felt surreal.

Someone who knew me of old would normally say, 'He's not that hard – I saw him crying in the playground once when a girl hit him.' Both sides were right; I was capable of having a fight now but I was also capable of being very soft. I never said that I was hard and I certainly never set out to be considered amongst the toughest in the school. I just wanted respect and to be left alone (not bullied) and by fighting back I achieved that goal. The thought of fighting back had been terrifying but like most things in life, the thought was far more frightening than actually doing it.

I look back at all of the things that happened to me way back then as a kid as being really good. Those events, although I didn't know it at the time, were to shape my future and help me to become the man I am today. So a big thank you to all the bullies in my life – your cowardly actions made me so much stronger. I now strongly believe that everything that happens, happens for a reason.

All of the hard and traumatic events in our lives are obstacles that we have to climb over. However, in doing so we shape our bodies and our personalities and so these events can only serve to make us stronger. It is a very hard concept to grasp, especially at times of struggle, but life will keep giving us obstacles in an effort to help us to grow stronger and survive. Stepping up to the terror barriers in my mind, pausing, and then nervously going forward into the middle of them has been one of the toughest things I have had to do in my life but also one of the most rewarding. Sometimes, when life seems to be dealing us a very hard hand, things might not make much sense. However, often when we look back over our lives we can join up the dots and it all makes sense as to why certain things happened when and how they did (not that this helps when you are in the middle of it).

After that first year school life settled down for me, confrontation-wise at least. In the second year

I had three fights or scuffles; in the third year, one fight, and in the whole of the remaining two years I only had one fight. I didn't need to fight – I was never a bully and everyone left me alone.

When I left school I got a job in a local factory, which I will talk about more in the next chapter.

Work meant that I had money in my pocket and enabled me to discover beer; I was out drinking most nights of the week. At weekends I got into lots of scrapes and punch-ups with my drinking buddies. To be honest, most of the fights were fuelled by drink; there was no courage involved, only the type to be found at the bottom of a beer glass. We used to joke that beer gave us beer muscles and they were very big.

We would all meet at the local pub and then head into Coventry town centre and usually end up in a mass brawl at the end of the night. At first these brawls were quite funny. We would meet up at our local pub on a Sunday morning to compare black eyes and split lips. However, as time moved on some of the fights took a turn for the worst. I can remember being in a few fights where things got so bad that no matter how much I had drunk, I sobered up pretty quickly. I saw people get glassed, men and women. I fought beside my friends after they had been glassed and were drenched in blood. Sometimes it looked as though their faces had been turned inside out and all the blood and skin tissue was on the outside, which was horrific to see. It certainly wasn't like the films, where people get bashed across the head then get up and walk away. People were being scarred for life, or even worse, killed. I can honestly say that in a lot of these situations I was terrified and not thinking about winning, just surviving. Fear was there in abundance.

One Christmas night I went for a few drinks with my girlfriend and wife to be, Bev, who was pregnant at the time. Bev and I left the pub early and walked back to my parents' house, which was close by and faced out on to a main road. We were relaxing in the house when I thought I heard a noise. It seemed to be coming from outside the front door, so I, being very brave (and probably a bit drunk), went to investigate and opened the door. Two lads who were obviously quite drunk were pissing up against the door and actually nearly pissed on my feet as I opened it. I felt a wave of anger rise up inside me. How dare they disrespect me and my parents' house? Not that they had a clue who I was or who my parents were. I could see that they were both very drunk but I was annoyed, so almost without thinking I gave the one nearest to me a back-handed slap across the face. Almost in an instant his friend pulled a knife. I was very angry but still knew not to challenge someone with a knife. He started shouting, 'Come on then, I'll stick you, you fucking twat.' I raced back into the kitchen, by which time my mum, dad and Bev were starting to look very worried, and pulled out a carving knife from the kitchen draw.

To be honest, by now my rational thinking was long gone. I reached the door and to my horror realised that the two lads were just a very small part of a much bigger drunken gang and they were all heading straight for me. I gestured with the knife as if to say 'Come on then', hoping that the size of the knife would scare them but the whole gang ran at me with drink-fuelled anger etched onto their distorted faces. At the last second I bottled it, stepped back into the house and tried to shut the front door but it was too late. I pushed against the door with all my strength as the gang pushed back. I was shitting myself. The door had a wooden panel at the bottom, the top half being made of glass. I looked at my parents and Bev; by now a look of terror was on their faces. As I tried desperately to close the door, hands, fists and feet were battering it from the other side. A beer bottle crashed through the glass and just missed my head. The sound of breaking glass, the shouts of anger and rage, the screams of terror from inside the house were deafening. What the fuck had I done? And what was about to happen? I couldn't hold them back much longer.

The gap between me and the door was getting wider, my strength was starting to wane. One of them poked his distorted, ugly face through the gap; I will never forget that face and the look of hatred on it. I wanted to punch him but I couldn't let go of the door. And then, silence... everything seemed to stop. I heard a commotion out in the street and very carefully and slowly opened the door. Some of my friends who I had been drinking with earlier in the night were walking home from the pub and saw the gang outside my house. As they walked across to see what was happening they saw one of the gang (it turned out to be the one I had slapped) throw a beer bottle through the window of my door. On seeing this my four friends tore wildly into the gang, throwing punches, kicks and headbutts, and actually knocked the bottle thrower unconscious. The other members of the gang were now under attack themselves, and even though they were greater in number they started to flee in several different directions.

When I realised what was happening I used the opportunity to reap my revenge. I punched one guy to the floor. As I did this I spotted the lad who had threatened me with the knife. We made eye contact for a split second and all I can think is that he saw the rage in my eyes and I saw fear in his. He started to run, with me in hot pursuit. I eventually caught him and started to give him a good hiding but I turned to see my friends still fighting back outside my house. I decided that this piece of shit could wait for another day. He was cowering like a baby so I gave him a few kicks and went back into the fray. My friend John pointed to a lad lying unconscious in the road and said, 'He is the one who smashed your window.'

All of my rational thinking was gone. I was enraged. How could anyone do this to my family, my parents, and the people I love more than anything else in the world? I started to kick him in the head. I am ashamed to say that I wanted to kill him and it was only Bev's and my mum's screams that stopped me.

A passing woman stopped to give him first aid. He was in a bad way but I did not care one little bit, I just wanted to kill him. The woman screamed that she was a nurse and that he was swallowing his tongue. My mum ran into the house, much to my disgust, and got a spoon so that they could hold his tongue in place.

Eventually an ambulance came and took him away. I found out later that he was OK.

This whole incident brought home to me just how pointless and bloody scary real violence is. All I can say is that anyone who glamorises violence has never experienced it; it is horrible and life changing. The rage I felt that night was scary. I could have easily killed someone and my whole life would have been completely different, and he would have lost his.

This was just one of several incidents that were a part of my life at this time. I saw some horrific injuries from glasses and knives and several times I thought I was a goner in fights. In hindsight I was probably just going to get a good kicking but when you are surrounded by drunken thugs slashing at you with bottles, glasses and whatever else they can get their hands on, it does feel as though you are going to die. Self-preservation becomes the order of the day.

These fights weren't like the ones at school. They were very nasty and could be very prolonged. There were no teachers to step in and break up the fights.

Around this time I was asked to work as a doorman at a rave club with some friends of mine. Once again this raised my self-doubts. I had to try to look cool on the outside but that little boy was still in me and he was most definitely scared. To be honest, most people at these raves were out of their heads on ecstasy tablets and God only knows what else. There was very little trouble, although there was always the threat of big drug dealers coming to the club to sort someone out. I heard lots of stories and saw some very strange goings-on behind the scenes but that's another story for another time.

By this time I was twenty-six years old, married to my beautiful wife Beverley and had two gorgeous children, Claire and Danny, who mean the world to me. Life was good but I still had this nagging fear of conflict. What if someone came into my life and challenged me and I bottled it, what would Bev and the kids think of me? What if I couldn't look after them? Would I lose them? People who knew me thought I was confident. I acted the part but that little boy was still there and he was still scared. I didn't feel like a real man, I felt like a little boy in a man's body, a fraud. I still had those old feelings of shame and of being a disappointment. Underneath all of my bravado, if the truth was known I still felt like a piece of crap just waiting to be found out for the fraud of a man that I was.

A good friend of mine, Tom Scott, was training with a martial artist called Geoff Thompson and said, 'Why don't you come along to his class?' I thought straight away, that's it, that's what I need, a black belt. I didn't care what system it was in, I just wanted a black belt and then people would see how tough I was and then no one would dare mess with me. I would have all the respect I craved.

I went along to Geoff's class and immediately liked the guy. He had a reputation as an up-and-coming doorman who took no prisoners but I just found him to be a gentleman. The club at the time was based around a karate system known as Shotokan. I had only been at the club a few weeks when someone asked Geoff how he felt as a nightclub doorman when he knew there was going to be trouble. His reply was like nectar to my ears, he said, 'I shit myself but I deal with it.' I had never heard anyone say this before, especially not a man, and what's more, a very hard man. I was relieved, I wasn't alone – even someone like Geoff Thompson gets scared. It felt as though a very heavy weight had been lifted off my shoulders.

In those days no one ever talked about feeling scared. In hindsight I guess everybody was scared but we all felt isolated with our feelings. I for one thought that I was the only person, at least amongst my friends and peers, who felt this level of fear.

I knew then that I just had to keep confronting my fears in the hope that it would get easier to live with them. After training with Geoff for around five years I achieved my black belt in Shotokan which felt great but to my bitter disappointment didn't help me with my fear of confrontation and this deep-seated insecurity about not being able to protect myself or my family. And of not being good enough, I actually felt as if I was more of a fraud now than before. Who was I to become a black belt? People were congratulating me on achieving the black belt grade but I felt dejected. Achieving the black belt turned out not to be the magic pill that I had hoped it would be. People would just expect more from me now and what if just like in the past I could not live up to their expectations? Those old feelings of shame, disappointment, rejection and oblivion were still hovering just above my head.

Geoff's reputation as a martial artist was growing rapidly. He was going to places like Las Vegas to train with the likes of TV star Chuck Norris. His own club was getting bigger; he was in every martial arts magazine and even on TV.

He came up with a training system called 'animal day', which was very controversial but also very cutting edge. Animal day was basically no-holds-barred sparring. This is common today with the advent of cage fighting but it was fairly new back then. It was all about pressure testing; Geoff's theory being that if you could stand the heat of the forge then you could mould yourself into anything that you wanted to be in life.

Geoff would ask for two volunteers to fight. He always asked for volunteers; that way you had to step forward into the arena. Then he would make you stand and face your opponent for what seemed like an eternity while he carried on speaking to the rest of the class, who by now were sitting around having formed a circle in which the fighters were to perform. Then, without warning, Geoff would say 'Go!'. And off we would go, tearing into each other until one of us couldn't carry on. I took part in lots of animal days and that did help me in my quest to conquer my fear of confrontation but I still had lots of fears and insecurities. No matter what I did my old insecurities refused to disappear. By this time I had also earned a black belt in ju-jitsu and had studied many other systems including boxing, judo, freestyle wrestling and Thai boxing.

Then in the very late nineties a new system called Vale Tudo came to Britain, which was to be the forerunner of the present-day cage fighting phenomenon. It was very controversial, so much so that the only local authority prepared to let a show go on in its area was Milton Keynes. People like Barry McGuigan (the boxing promoter) were on television saying it was barbaric and should be banned everywhere. All I can say to that is I would rather enter a Vale Tudo competition than try to go ten rounds with him. Because of the fearsome reputation of Geoff's club some of us were asked to fight on a Vale Tudo bill. I jumped at the chance; after all, it was another opportunity to face my fears.

I remember waking up from a deep sleep in the middle of the night a few days before my fight. I had an overwhelming feeling of distraught fear, panic, dread and many more unpleasant emotions racing through my body. My heart was pounding and I was drenched in sweat. I really felt as though I couldn't go through with the fight. The more I thought about it the worse my fear became. My mind was running away with me, it didn't make sense; I was in a full-blown panic and getting worse by the second. I hovered over the phone, debating if I should call Geoff Thompson and tell him I was pulling out of the fight. It was three o'clock in the morning and I was feeling very alone and very scared, my fears seemed to be coming at me from every direction: fear of failure, fear of not being good enough, fear of losing face, fear of looking an idiot, fear of not being a man. How had I managed to get myself in to such a mess? Why had I agreed to have this fight?

I turned on the radio (which I don't normally do at three o'clock in the morning) and Robbie Williams' song, 'Angels', was playing. As I listened to the words 'giving love and protection' I started to feel better and gradually calmed down. I asked myself, 'What's the worst that could happen?' Listening to that song allowed me to change from a state of panic to one of calmness; this was to be a valuable lesson. I realised that by changing my focus or perception I could actually change my feelings, a useful fact for us all to be aware of.

That night was a very uncomfortable one, but I have learned over the years that the more uncomfortable I am, the more I grow. The bigger the battle, the bigger the rewards. I learned that what you focus on will grow. I was focusing on fighting in front of 2,000 people against an opponent I didn't know. I did know he had fought at this venue before and in this system and I hadn't. I had also damaged my ankle and this was playing on my mind. In short, I was focusing on all the negative aspects of the fight. This brought me right into the emotional side of my brain.

Keeping this really simple, there is a theory in psychiatry that says the left side of the brain is logical and the right side is emotional. I was embedded in the emotional side of my brain and getting a massive burst of fear accompanied by its faithful sidekicks, adrenalin and cortisol, which were causing my heart rate to increase and making me sweat profusely. To put it mildly, I was in a really uncomfortable emotional state, in fact, I was a wreck.

The Robbie Williams record fortunately broke that state and I started to switch from the emotional side of my brain to the rational side. I began asking myself questions like, what's the worst that can happen? How hard have you trained for this? Look who you have trained with, they are all legends. I changed my focus and felt much better.

I actually lost the fight and was very disappointed at the time. I lost the fight due to in-fight adrenalin that caused me to lose concentration and hence get submitted.

Fear is a very powerful adversary; it's not just about facing it or climbing into the ring. It's about continuously facing it, again and again, because it will try to sneak back in to your mind at every opportunity. I entered a second contest and lost that also and decided to retire from heavy sparring and fighting as it was ruining my good looks.

What I did achieve, though, and I didn't quite realise this at the time, was that at long last I had overcome my fear of confrontation and in the process of doing so, I felt one hell of a lot less insecure. By facing my fear year after year and in the most confrontational ways I had finally learned how to control it; not make it go away, but control it. We are all different and for me to win this battle I had to keep having it over and over again until I learned the lessons that I personally needed to learn. Having won my personal battle with confrontation I no longer felt the need to have it in my life. I often wondered whether my fear attracted the very thing that I was afraid of into my life and now that I was no longer scared that attraction had disappeared.

I also realised that I had subconsciously set a goal of just getting into the ring and not even thought about winning. I was so scared of getting in there that just to step into that arena was a success to me. I had not even thought about winning, just taking part, which was another valuable lesson.

In hindsight if I had set my goal higher and on winning and not just taking part, I could have been a champion. But then again, hindsight is a wonderful thing.

I now train and teach for fun. I am a 5th Dan martial artist with the British Combat System. I run my own self-defence organisation with my good friend Matty Evans called the Real Combat System. I love training and teaching, especially if there is no ego involved, and I can laugh and train at the same time.

At this point I have to go back to my dog, Duke. He was the first dog that I ever owned; before I got him I read as many books on dog training as I could. I took lots of advice from other dog owners but it wasn't until I actually took him out into the real world and started to train him that I really learned what training a dog is all about. It took me eighteen frustrating months to turn him into a brilliant and obedient dog. There were many times in those eighteen months that I prematurely thought, I've got him trained now, we are there. Then he would run after another dog or not come back when I called him. It always felt after a setback like this as if we were starting all over again. I know that this wasn't the case but that is how it felt. I don't believe that we ever slip back to where we started. Once we have learned a lesson, it cannot be unlearned.

It was very much like this with my fear of confrontation, going right back to my dad taking me boxing, my school friends ignoring me in the street. The school bullies, the school fights, the drunken fights, my black belts. The animal days and finally the no-holds-barred tournaments. What a journey, only to end up in a way back where I started, with the realisation that fear is natural we are born with it; everybody has it, no matter how much they deny it. It has been my companion all through my life, only now, very much like my dog, it is obediently walking beside me on a lead. It hasn't gone, it's still with me, only now I feel that I have it under a greater degree of control.

There are no shortcuts, no secrets – you have to do the work. The walls of fear are a good thing; in climbing them you get stronger, conditioned, tougher and more importantly, enlightened. The lessons have to be learned on the inside. Life's events give us the opportunities to challenge the beliefs that we have formed about ourselves. To change those beliefs takes a shift of consciousness. Once you realise that it is you who chooses how to feel and once you take the responsibility for your own actions and the choices that you make, then the world will become your oyster. You are a creator, so why not start creating?

THE RESCUER

Ileft school at sixteen not really knowing what career path I wanted to follow. I hadn't done particularly well in my exams, getting just below average results in my CSEs. The careers teacher told me that I should aim for a career in something like carpet fitting, or fitting double glazing. In other words, a semi-skilled job. My parents and in particular my dad had always stressed the importance of getting an apprenticeship. 'Get an apprenticeship and you will never be out of work,' was my dad's advice. 'It doesn't matter what the apprenticeship is in, just get one.' So the expectations of me were to follow in my father's footsteps (he was a bricklayer) in the building industry or any industry as long as it included an apprenticeship.

Any parents reading this book need to be aware of how important expectations are because there is a very good chance that your children will at least try to meet your expectations of them, whether they are low or high. My parents probably grew up and met the expectations of their parents and these expectations were now being passed on to me! I was from a working-class background and so had working-class expectations. By the way, I am not saying there is anything wrong with having working-class expectations. I am just saying that is the way it was. I see families who have very low expectations of their children and the children grow up to meet those low expectations, often leading a life of crime, and they in turn pass those expectations on to their own offspring. Once in a while someone will realise what is happening and change their expectations. This can break the cycle, which is very hard to do (we are back to the pike story again – conditioning) but when it happens it is great to see.

There have even been experiments where classes full of so-called under-achieving students were placed under the supervision of teachers who were lied to and told that they would be teaching high achievers. Because the teachers had high expectations of the pupils, their pass rates improved dramatically.

Even more important than other people's expectations of you are the expectations that you have of yourself. Look at your life now – are you happy? Are you doing the things that you want to do? Do you feel that you are roughly where you deserve to be or where you expected yourself to be at this time in your life? Did you ever really expect to do any better? If you are not happy with your answers to these questions, don't be discouraged; it's not too late to change your future. You just have to change your expectations.

After leaving school at sixteen I attended literally hundreds of tests for various apprenticeships. Coventry still had lots of factories (we are talking pre-Thatcher years here). I received rejection letter after rejection letter. My dad worked at a factory called British Celanese and suggested that I tried there, which I duly did. He never said anything but I guess he pulled a few strings because I was accepted for an apprenticeship as a pipe-fitter welder. I had gone to the job interview thinking that I was applying for a position as an apprentice electrician. I had never even heard of a pipe-fitter welder, but it was an apprenticeship and to be honest, the way things were looking on the job front, I didn't think that I would be offered anything else, so I gratefully accepted it.

I don't suppose I will ever know for sure but I think they gave me the job because of my dad. He was the type of man who always worked hard and never had a day off unless he was genuinely sick; he had to be really ill to miss work.

Unfortunately for them, I wasn't like my dad. I failed the first two years of my apprenticeship and had to re-sit the exams. I was given a final warning for losing time and being late too often. At the end of my four-year apprenticeship the recession was in full bloom. Most of the apprentices who finished that year had the dubious honour of being the first ever apprentices to be made jobless in the history of British Celanese and I was one of them. I didn't care – I had grown bored of pipe-fitting and welding and besides, I had an apprenticeship now; I would never be out of work. I went to every pipe-fitter welding company in Coventry and they all said the same thing. It used to go something like this:

'Hello, my name is Anthony Somers. I see you have a pipe-fitting job advertised and I am interested.'

'What experience have you got?'

'I have got an apprenticeship.'

'Yes, but what experience have you got?'

'I have got a four-year apprenticeship.'

'Look, mate, a four-year apprenticeship is great, well done, but it doesn't count as experience, so sorry, I can't offer you anything, come back when you have got some experience.'

How was I supposed to get experience when no one would give me a job?

I gave up on pipe-fitting and messed about for the next two years doing cash-in-hand work, like working on market stalls or labouring for people. One of my worst jobs was welding aluminium buckets that were used to store meat. The stench of burning, rotting meat was horrendous; I can still recall it now and it still makes my stomach turn. It was the middle of a bitterly cold winter, we worked in a big shed, there was no heating and it was so cold that at the end of the day I would go home and sit by the fire until my skin was burning, but the cold had gone right through to my bones and I couldn't get warm no matter what I did – and all for £10 a day, which was crap even back then.

I went on welding courses to improve my chances of getting work but it was always the same story – good qualifications but not enough experience. I decided to start at the bottom and went for a welding job that involved really basic work, sitting at a bench all day welding brackets together (how boring). When I walked into the factory it was like walking into a morgue. The foreman showed me around and told me I would be sitting at a designated bench (I was lucky I was getting my own bench). My job would entail welding brackets and bosses in a jig for eight hours a day. I smiled but on the inside I was thinking, is this it? Is this all that I deserve? Is this my future? I asked him how much I would be paid; he said £100 per week. This was really poor money.

I knew that this was going to be a crap job and I was prepared to do it but not for a pittance. So I told him that I would do the job but not at that rate of pay, I wanted more. He was shocked but said, 'Let me go and call my boss.' He came back a few minutes later and said, 'The boss will go to £105 per week.' Once again I said thanks but no thanks. Off he went to make another call to his boss. He came back and looked really nervous. 'The boss is coming down to see you himself.' I waited a few more minutes and then in walked the boss; he was a big red-faced guy with a full ginger beard. He reminded me of one of those roughneck characters that you see in old western films; he was quite an intimidating character. He asked me to follow him, which I did.

We walked back up to the welding area of the factory where he asked me how much money I would want to work there. I didn't want to be too greedy so I said I would take £125 per week, which still wasn't great but it was getting better. His chin nearly hit the floor and his face turned an even deeper crimson colour. I could tell he wasn't pleased. He said, 'See him over there,' and pointed at a guy with permed blond hair and a gormless look on his face. 'He has worked here for three years and gets a hundred and ten pounds a week and see him over there—' he pointed at a slightly older guy who looked like he had a bit more about him —'he is my top welder and he only gets £125 per week.' He looked at me, waiting for an answer. I just shrugged my shoulders as if to say 'tough shit'. He was really fuming now. I got the feeling that he would have loved to punch me, but fair play to him he held it together and just said, 'You had better leave.' I turned to walk away, taking one last look at the two welders. The blond-haired one was flabbergasted. He shook his head and looked at me in amazement as if to say, 'You idiot, what have you done? This is a great job, you should be grateful for the opportunity.' The other guy just bowed his head and looked slightly ashamed; he knew that I had done the right thing. I didn't belong there but the sad thing was, neither did he.

After this episode I decided that I would do any type of work that came along, as long as it paid the bills. I worked in a brickyard making bricks for a year. I worked in factories doing various types of mostly monotonous work. I even worked as a pipe-fitter's mate; they said I didn't have enough experience to work as a pipe-fitter but my apprenticeship was enough for them to allow me to work as a labourer.

Around this time I met Beverley, fell in love and my life changed in a big way.

We had our beautiful daughter Claire and bought our first house for £11,950, which was a lot of money to us. Working as a pipe-fitter's mate wasn't exactly great money. One Christmas, Bev had to ask her dad to help us financially as the gas people were threatening to cut us off for an unpaid bill. It wasn't as if we were extravagant; the house was so cold that on some mornings there would be ice on the insides of the windows as well as out. There was no central heating, just a couple of small gas fires to keep us warm. But I have to say these were happy times; we were very much in love.

When Claire was born, although I was very happy, as most new fathers are, I also felt a weight of responsibility start to form around my neck. I had a partner and a newborn baby to provide for. Now, in hindsight, I know that I placed that weight around my own neck but trust me, it still felt heavy at the time. My old fears of not being good enough were resurfacing. I didn't feel good enough as a partner, let alone a father. I wasn't earning much money and felt as though I was letting my new family down. My wife having to ask her dad for money to pay our bills did very little for my fragile ego.

I went from job to job in search of better money. One day my father-in-law said, 'Why don't you apply for a job at the Peugeot car factory? I hear that they are doing very well and are starting another shift and the money's not bad.'

I duly applied and got the job; yes, it was more money but I hated the place from the time I first walked through the big rusty entrance gates. I was placed on a track doing the same spot welding job, minute after minute, hour after hour for forty hours a week. It was mind-numbingly boring. I met some nice people in there but almost all they did was moan about the factory and how shit it was to be working there and I had to agree.

After I had been at the factory for about a year there was a big announcement. The company was doing so well that they were starting a new night shift. What's more, everybody was going to have to work nights; we were not given a choice, just told, 'Be grateful that you have a job.' From now on we would have to do a month of day shifts followed by a month of night shifts. I could not believe what I was hearing. It was bad enough being there all day, let alone having to be there all night. I was devastated; my life would consist of working all night and sleeping all day. I couldn't even call that a life. At around this time I put my thoughts down on some paper and this is what I came up with, which really summed up my feelings:

```
Another nauseating Monday morning,
the worst day of what would surely
be another nauseating week of tedious
factory life. I walked down the long
grey cold concrete drive as slowly as
I could, being careful not to trip
over my chin as it scraped dejectedly
before me. I noticed my old friend the
dark cloud had claimed his rightful
place and was hovering just above my
```

head. Everyone who works here has one, it comes with the job; it's like a faithful yet imaginary friend who you just know will be patiently waiting at the gate for you every morning.

The line of men waiting to clock in reminded me of those poor sad creatures that you see on the telly; you know, the ones in the slaughterhouse waiting for the inevitable act to happen. They must know what is coming, they must have at least an inkling, and yet they still obediently wait in line.

As I approached the clock I could hear it ticking loudly, tick tic, tick tock, tick tic, just as it always did. It seemed to be abrasively and impatiently saying, 'Come on, hurry up, I haven't got all day you know.' I put my time card into the slot. Was it my imagination or did the clock's hands actually start to slow down? I was in and I knew that seconds would seem like minutes and minutes would seem like hours.

As the clock viciously punched its holes into my card, the thud of its mechanisms reminded me of the sound that rusty old prison gates make as they slam shut and trap the condemned inmates inside their walls. I felt trapped, smothered, although I knew in reality these traps that felt like

chains and bars were all in my head.
But what could I do? I had a wife and
two small children to look after; it
wasn't my fault, was it?

I walked through the factory to my
position on the dreaded track with my
dark cloud in tow. At first glance into
the interior of the factory it looked
as though a giant robotic spider had
haphazardly spun its steel web over
everything in sight. Metal girders and
concrete beams seemed to be scattered
everywhere. There were pulleys and
chains and bundles of brightly coloured
wires weaving in and out of every
orifice. Row upon row of machinery
stood to attention and glistened in the
glare of artificial lights. However,
at a second glance you could tell
that there was a distinct order to
this chaos. All of the machines were
placed strategically around what was
the heart of the factory, the dreaded
track! The track weaved its way right
through the centre of the factory and,
it seemed, right through the centre of
our lives. Once started it could never
be stopped or even slowed down, no
matter what the circumstances.

I took up my position, just pausing
to check that my dark cloud was still
in place (no need to worry, of course
- it was). I then took a deep breath
of the damp and musky air. The smell

of oil, sweat and depression filled my
nostrils. I prayed to myself, please
God, please let this be the day that
the track stops, blows up - who cares,
please! The piercing shrill of the
whistle sounded and right on cue the
factory burst into life. The track
creaked, moaned and then laboriously
started to move. The sound of metal
hitting metal filled the air. The arc
welders struck up their arcs, causing
the atmosphere to light up with row
after row of shooting yellow and blue
sparks. The smell of burning filled the
great halls as clouds of smoke descended
on to the helpless workers below.

I started my mundane spot welding job
and my mind went into its usual trance-
like state. Now I was on an exotic beach,
glass of cold beer in hand, surrounded
by the most beautiful topless women. I
let the sun's hot rays soothe my aching
body as at the same time the cool sea
breeze refreshed me. The sea gently
lapped against the sand and the palm
trees danced in the cool breeze. No
artist could ever capture the beauty
of this place and no poet could ever
find the words to describe it; it was
my sanctuary, paradise. The piercing
shrill of the break-time whistle brought
me crashing back to reality.

I sat in the canteen eating my cheese
and pickle sandwiches. (Never tell

your wife you like a certain type of
sandwich - you will get them forever
and when you moan about it she will
say, 'But you said you liked them.'
Yeah, but that was six months ago,
love!) I was listening to the same
old boring conversations. They always
started with what was on telly last
night. It seemed to me that they
hated the telly. 'It was crap, same
old stuff, repeats, why do we pay
our bloody licence fees?' And yet
they seemed to watch everything that
there was to watch. They could tell
you every character in every soap and
sitcom. Then they would moan about
their wives and how their wives never
stopped moaning. They hated their sex
lives, mainly because their sex lives
were non-existent. I wondered if they
had ever thought about turning off
the telly and talking to their wives.
But then what would they have to talk
about? Their shitty jobs or even maybe
what they were missing on the telly.
Then came the biggest and by far, in
my eyes, the most annoying moan of
all. They hated the factory, that was
obvious, but they would say, 'If only
I had my time over again, things would
be different.' This life was all they
had known; they could leave at any
time, but would they? No way. Just
at that moment a terrifying thought
hit me: if I stayed here, I would end
up like them. I was looking into the

future, my future, and I didn't like
it one little bit.

A silent but deafening scream filled
my head. I looked up and my dark cloud
thickened. Suddenly, perhaps out of
desperation, an inner strength that
I had never experienced before shot
through my body like a speeding bullet.
It was decision time. I could stay
here and accept my fate or I could
take control of my own destiny. My
past decisions had taken me to this
factory and I knew that the decisions
I made now would shape my future.

I had always wanted to become a firefighter,
but could I do it? Was I good enough? I had to
try. The rest of the day was spent planning my
escape. I decided to study and start a new fitness
regime. I felt like a little kid. As well as a goal and
a dream, I also had a fear to motivate me. The
fear was of spending the next forty years of my
life staring at that nauseating, soul-destroying
track. I looked up; my cloud was now a paler
grey and much smaller, I could see the sun's rays
through the skylights in the factory roof and I
was on my way!

I realised that I wasn't going to get out of this life
alive and I wanted to make the best of the time
I had left. I didn't want to sit and bitch or moan
for the next forty years – it was time to change.

I asked myself if I could do any job in the world, what would it be? The answer that came in to my mind, and I could not tell you why, was to be a firefighter. I liked the thought of racing around on fire engines, running into burning buildings and saving people. I imagined myself as a hero with my picture on the front pages of the national press for my heroic deeds.

I now had an achievable goal to aim for and one that filled me with excitement, I was raring to go. I was inspired to take action and make big changes.

Within a few days of writing my thoughts down I had applied for several other jobs, one of which was as a firefighter. I didn't know how long the process of getting into the fire service would take, that was if I was even lucky enough to get in, so I covered my options by applying for other work. I eventually ended up doing five months of night shifts at Peugeot which, to put it mildly, I really did not enjoy. One of the jobs I had applied for accepted my application, so I left Peugeot and started work as a fabricator welder for a company that made forklift trucks. As factory jobs go it wasn't too bad, I was left alone to get on with my work.

There was plenty of overtime if I wanted it and it was day shifts only, thankfully. I settled into my new job and actually started to like it; the money was about the same as I was on at Peugeot but we finished early on a Friday, the bonus being that I could work Friday afternoon and Saturday morning as overtime, which was time and a half, so financially things were improving.

The down side to earning the extra money through overtime was that when things went quiet, the overtime stopped. By now my son Danny had been born and we needed the extra money that the overtime brought in. When the overtime was not available, I ended up working in the factory all day, getting the bus home (I had to sell my old banger of a car to pay some bills), quickly eating my tea and then running to the local Sainsbury's store and packing shelves until ten o'clock at night.

However, I still had this dream of being a firefighter. I had queued up with literally hundreds of other people to get an application form as soon as the job applications were announced in the local paper. I filled it in as quickly as possible, sent it off, and impatiently waited to hear back from them. I had been told that only four out of every one hundred people who applied were successful in gaining entry to the service.

My intent to get out of the factory was at such a high level that if only one out of every hundred people who applied was accepted, I was determined to be that one. I had also heard from different sources that to improve my slim chances of getting into the service I would have to be very fit as the physical tests to gain entry were very tough. I would also, to my horror, have to be good at maths for the written entry exam.

On the fitness side I was already doing martial arts with Geoff Thompson but I knew this wouldn't be enough, so I joined a boxing class – not because I wanted to box but because I knew from past experience that the training was very tough.

The days I wasn't boxing or at my martial arts class I was out running. My biggest dread was the maths part of the test. At school I had really struggled with maths. It was a subject that I hated and had basically dismissed as being irrelevant but now it was proving to be very relevant to my life.

I decided to start again, after all, the past was the past, so I went along to WHSmith and purchased a very basic maths book.

When I say basic, that is exactly what I mean – on the first page it had a diagram of a circle and said, 'This is a circle. Cut it down the middle and you will have two halves. Cut the two halves in half and you will have four quarters.' Every dinner time and break time I would sit in my welding booth, eating my cheese and pickle sandwiches and working my way through the book. The guy in the next welding booth was great at maths and whenever I got stuck, which was often the case, he would take great delight in putting me right.

I eventually received a letter telling me that my application form had been accepted and I was to attend the fire service headquarters in Birmingham for a written test.

On a cold winter's morning I sat in a dull, grey room with about forty other people and waited for the test papers to be handed out. To say I was nervous and not very confident would be the understatement of the year. Why hadn't I listened to my mum and studied harder at school? Why hadn't I listened to all of my old maths teachers?

The test was under way and I wrote my answers as quickly as I could. We were being timed, so I decided to focus on the questions that I felt I could answer first and ignored the rest. The whole test was split into three sections: maths, English and mechanical equations, which was basically questions like, 'If I turn this pulley this way, what effect will it have on the gear system two miles further down the line?' In-between each section there was a short break but nobody spoke. I guess we were all nervous and just wanted to get on with it.

At the end of the test I just sat there feeling pretty dejected. I didn't think I had done very well and was thinking about heading back to the factory the next day. I also imagined myself returning home and telling my wife that I had failed. I had tried my best but as usual it just wasn't good enough. One of the ladies who had been handing out the test papers came back into the room; she announced that she would be calling out a list of names. All of those people whose names were called would be asked to leave the room. My name wasn't on the long list that she called out. There were about twelve of us left. She left the room and returned after a few minutes. I thought, here we go – the ones who have been called out have passed and those of us still sitting here have failed. She then said with a big smile on her face, 'You have all passed and unfortunately those asked to leave have failed.' I could have screamed with joy. I wanted to hug her but I just sat there frozen in my chair. I had passed, I was on my way!! I felt as though I could have run all the way home to Coventry (it was a good 20 miles). I was over the moon.

Next to come was the physical test and this had a reputation for being brutal; the vast majority of applicants didn't make it past this bit. The test was set out over two days – the first day was at Bickenhill fire station near Birmingham airport and the second was at fire service headquarters, where I had taken the written test.

I attended Bickenhill fire station along with around fifty other applicants on a warm summer's day in 1989. We were all told to dress in firefighter uniforms, which consisted of yellow plastic leggings, a very thick tunic, a yellow helmet and rubber boots. The first thing I noticed was how hot I felt in all that gear. It was great to look and feel like a real firefighter but boy was it going to be hard work. We were split into groups by a sergeant-major-type officer and then the groups were led off to do different tasks. My group's first task was to climb up a 9-metre ladder that was pitched up to a third-floor window on what is known in the fire service as a drill tower. Drill towers are used to practise pitching different sized ladders and working at heights.

My first task was to climb to just below the top of the ladder, put one leg through the rounds of the ladder and then lean back as far as I could, letting go of the ladder and being held in position by my one leg through the rounds.

I had one problem with this part of the test – I wouldn't say I had a real phobia of heights but I was certainly very uncomfortable with them and especially ladders. However, I wasn't going to let a little bit of fear stop me now. So off I went up the ladder, shitting myself on the inside but trying to look like Cool Hand Luke on the outside. I climbed the ladder as quickly as I could and placed my size ten foot awkwardly through the rounds and leaned back until the officer at the bottom shouted 'OK!', and then I made my way back down, still trying to look cool and praying that no one would see how hard my heart was pounding or how rapidly my legs were shaking.

Next, we were shown how to ship a hydrant lid and fit a stand pipe onto it and turn it on. Hydrants, for those who don't know, is under the steel lids you see on pavements and in roads and are used by firemen to fill up their fire engines with water. We had to remove the steel lids, attach a stand pipe to the hydrant and turn it on as quickly as possible while constantly being shouted at by the training officers. I didn't find this bit too hard, although some people seemed to struggle and kept dropping pieces of equipment. I think this was mainly due to the deliberate pressure being applied to them by the training officers. I guess if you were the nervous type this was where they were going to find out.

The next test was inside the building and was called the step test. This involved stepping up onto a box and back down again to a set beat for five minutes. The idea of this test wasn't exactly to tire us out, although it was tiring; the idea was to check our recovery rates. So our pulse was taken before we started, then when we finished and then after another minute to see how quickly our pulses returned to normal. The lady who checked my pulse actually commented on how good it was and how fit I must be, which did my self-confidence no harm whatsoever (all that tough boxing training was paying off).

We were halfway through the day now and back out in the drill yard dressed in our full fire kit. The next task and by far the hardest physically was about to begin under the glare of the shining sun. We had to take a length of tightly coiled yellow hose and stand on the loose end. We then had to lift the hose using both hands and hold it straight out in front of us. The idea was to run, unravelling the hose as we went along. By standing on the loose end you ensured that one end of the hose remained in the starting position, which was the whole idea. At a real fire hundreds of these lengths of hose could be joined together so that water could be taken from one place to another; for example, from a river to a fire a mile away. This was a really awkward exercise. As well as being quite heavy the hose was 25 metres in length. My first few attempts saw me run like mad, then realise I hadn't stood on the loose end of the hose, so all I was doing was carrying the hose out in front of me and not leaving any behind. The training officers thought that this was hilarious; the saving grace for me was that I wasn't alone, quite a few of the others were doing the same thing and some were even tripping over the hose and getting into a real tangled mess.

After a few test runs we were all lined up across the drill yard and told to run out the hose as we had been shown and then roll it back up to its original coiled position as fast as we could and keep doing this until we were told to stop.

Remembering to stand on one end of the hose and then running and spinning the remaining coil of hose out at the same time was hard enough. However, what was even harder was when you reached the end of the hose, you had to turn around and roll it all back up again. To do this meant being almost in a crouching position, which was torture on the thighs, and all the time we were being ordered and shouted at to work faster and harder. I was sweating like a pig, cursing the sun and the heavy firefighter's uniform, and to make it worse everyone seemed to be going faster than I was. There was no rest; the idea was to keep going until they told us to stop.

Gradually I noticed people start to pull up and either just walk off the yard or sit down when they had obviously had enough. I kept going, even though my legs were under tremendous strain and felt like two pieces of jelly. I knew that I was slowing down but I wouldn't stop. The negative voices in my head were saying, 'Look, just stop, you're knackered. It's not that bad, loads of people have stopped, you're not on your own.' I thought of the night shifts at Peugeot and of how hard I had trained for this, the embarrassment of buying a child's maths book. 'NO!' I wasn't giving in, fuck that. Then, after what seemed like an eternity, came the order to stop. My arms ached, my legs were shaking virtually uncontrollably and I couldn't straighten my back from being in a crouched position. I looked around and was surprised to see that there were only about eight of us left; well over half the other applicants had gone. That exercise had really taken its toll on my fellow applicants but I was still there. 'YES!! YOU BEAUTY!'

After getting showered and drinking vast amounts of water to rehydrate we were told to sit in a large office and wait for a senior officer to come and talk to us. Eventually three officers came into the room. The leader told us to relax as we had all passed the first day of the practical test and that this was just an informal chat. He then proceeded to tell us that he had our original application forms and just wanted to ask us a few questions in an attempt to get to know us a bit better. He went around the room in a relaxed manner asking people about things they had written on their forms. When he got to me he said, 'Mr Somers, I see you do some charity work, what exactly is it that you do?'

Shit! It had been about eighteen months since I had filled in that form and I couldn't remember what I had said, but one thing was certain – I definitely didn't do any charity work. I said the first thing that came into my head: 'Yes, sir, I am very religious and every Sunday at church I always help the priest by taking the collection plate around the congregation.' Out of the corner of my eye I saw a black lad smile and lower his head; he knew and I knew and I guess everyone else in the room knew I had just spouted a load of complete bullshit. I felt myself going red and felt very embarrassed at my pathetic answer but the officer quickly moved on.

He asked the next guy, 'Why do you want to join the fire service?'

This guy seemed nice enough but just a little bit cocky. 'I want to join the fire service for the money. I don't really care about the job, it's just good money.' I was surprised at his answer, not just the way he said it in a very cocky tone but because I thought the money wasn't that good; in fact, I would be taking a pay cut if I was accepted into the service. Not that it mattered what we said anyway, because this was an informal chat and we had all passed. We were than told that we could leave and to turn up at fire service headquarters at ten o'clock in a week's time.

As we got up to leave the officer asked the guy who had been a bit cocky to stay behind. The black guy who had smiled at the thought of me bringing the collection plate around the church on a Sunday morning turned to me and said, 'We won't see him again.' I was surprised. 'What do you mean? We have all passed, that wasn't part of the test.' He just said, 'From the time you step into this station you are being watched and assessed; trust me, we won't see him again.' I was shocked, partly at my own naivety, but he was right; I never did see that lad again.

The second part of the test was a week later; I was at fire service headquarters in Birmingham and, as usual, nice and early. There was about thirty of us there and everybody looked very nervous. We were given a quick tour of the station, which we were informed was one of the busiest fire stations in the West Midlands. We were then split into three groups of ten and the groups were separated from each other. Eventually my group was called; we once again had to dress in firefighter's uniform. We were then led into a small room with a very strong smell of disinfectant. One by one we were told to try on a breathing apparatus face mask. These are normally attached to an air supply and firefighters use them in order to breathe when they enter buildings on fire to search for people and indeed put out the fires. They are probably one of the most, if not the most, important pieces of equipment in a firefighter's life. A training officer explained how the masks worked and how they were to be worn. For this part of the test there would be no air supply fitted to the mask. It was still possible to breathe but to get a decent breath you had to suck really hard; basically, our breathing would be severely restricted.

The training officer put the mask over my face and pulled the adjusting straps tight. I felt a wave of panic sweep through my body, and I felt as though I couldn't breathe. I wanted to tear the mask off. Shit! I was claustrophobic. I knew that if I tore the mask off my face I would fail but the feeling of panic was intense. I felt my hands rise towards the mask as if acting of their own accord. The mask was by now steamed up with my hot breath and I couldn't see a thing. I started to talk to myself, my inner voice was in overdrive:

'I can't breathe.'
  'You can breathe.'
  'I can't, I can't, I'm going to die.'
  'Right, calm down. Look – you are still standing and so is everyone else. You can breathe, don't be stupid. If they can do it then so can you, just relax your breathing. That's it, look, you can do this, now just get on with it, and keep breathing.'

I relaxed and monitored my breathing. It was hard to breathe but the fact that I was still conscious was proof enough that I could do it. The training officer then shouted, 'Right, form a line and put your hand on the shoulder of the person in front of you and follow me.' I put my hand on the shoulder of the guy in front and the line started to move forward. The guy in line behind me gripped my shoulder; I could feel the tension through his tight grip. My mask was so badly steamed up that I couldn't see a thing. I held on to the guy in front's shoulder as tightly as I could. We shuffled along very slowly and carefully. I sensed through the change in light that we had left the building and were outside. Then the light was gone and we were in darkness. The atmosphere changed. There was lots of shouting going on in front of me. I couldn't see and my hearing senses were in overdrive.

I was suddenly and roughly pulled forward. 'Right, we are going to give you this barrel full of water. Whatever you do, don't let go of it or you will fail.' The barrel was thrust into my arms; I cradled it against my chest, it felt very heavy and very awkward to hold but no matter what, I was not going to let it go. I was then pushed forward and told to run. I stumbled but stayed on my feet and lurched forward. I felt as though I could hardly breathe through the face mask, I was hot, scared and worst of all I couldn't see a bloody thing. The training officers were continually pushing me and shouting non-stop. 'Come on, hurry up, faster! Is that all you've got? You've got to do better than this. So you want to be a firefighter, do you?' I was pushed forward again. The barrel was getting heavier and heavier but I wouldn't let it go.

Then my head was pushed down and I was forced to crawl through what felt like a concrete tunnel. I had to push the barrel in front of me as the tunnel was very narrow; basically, it was a case of shuffling using my elbows and knees to get some purchase on the sides. Then, suddenly, the barrel started to fall. I was at the end of the tunnel but I wouldn't let go. With a big effort I pushed forward and, still holding onto the barrel, followed it to the floor. I was then hauled to my feet and told to carry on; once again I stumbled forward through what felt like a series of concrete tunnels. One minute I would be running, barrel in hand, the next minute I would be crawling, barrel in hand. This just seemed to go on and on forever. At one point someone shouted, 'Keep running, that's one circuit completed.' I wondered how many circuits there would be, how long would this last? I was absolutely knackered but I would not give in so off I went again.

Every now and again as I crawled through the tunnels I would get a sense of someone in front of me or behind me. As I gulped in my big breaths I would hear them breathing or shuffling or getting shouted at; I wasn't going through this alone. As I stumbled forward after what seemed once again like an eternity I heard someone in front of me shout, 'That's two circuits.' I was then abruptly stopped by what felt like a giant hand gripping my shoulder. I heard voices in front of me. 'Do you want to carry on?' What sounded like a frail and exhausted voice replied, 'No, sir.' Then there was silence. I was suddenly pushed forward. Once again I stumbled and headed for the floor, by now almost too weak to stand. I was running, or should I say walking, on empty, I was exhausted. Just before I fell, almost letting go of the barrel, two hands gripped me and then I heard the same voice say to me, 'Do you want to carry on?' I felt beaten, defeated, I was exhausted and had nothing left, my whole body ached, my arms were numb from holding onto this stupid barrel. I wanted to say no; after all, the guy in front had said no, I wouldn't be alone. I knew that if I said no, I wanted to stop, that I would fail but I didn't care anymore. Every part of me wanted to stop, to give in, I was completely exhausted.

I was about to say no when from somewhere deep down inside of me the words 'Yes, sir!' came up and out of my mouth. Before I could pause for breath I was pushed forward again and headed off for my third circuit of pain. I had only run a few more feet when once again I was abruptly grasped and then pushed through a door and emerged out of the darkness into daylight. I was told to put my barrel down and to remove my face mask. I gladly dropped the barrel but I just didn't have the energy to undo my face mask, I had no strength left. The training officer undid the straps on my mask, smiled at me and said, 'Well done, you have just passed the hardest part of the test.' I felt relieved but I was too tired to even return his smile. He led me back to the changing rooms and gave me some water while at the same time explaining that the reason they asked if we wanted to stop during the test was to see if we had the will power to keep going. They knew that we were exhausted but those who had said yes, they wanted to stop, were just a few feet away from passing. I felt genuinely sorry for the guy in front of me who had stopped. I knew how he must have felt; just like the pike, all he had to do was give it one more go. I was so close to stopping myself but I was still here and starting to feel very proud of myself.

This was a fantastic lesson for me about not giving in. I don't know where that little voice that said yes came from. It could have been my guardian angel, it could have been God, I don't know, but I am so glad it was there and I am so glad that I listened and I never gave up.

Only five of us managed to pass that part of the test and after getting showered and changed we were given the final task of the day. We were shown how to tie a knot around a piece of pipe and then had to demonstrate that we could take in the information that we had been shown and repeat the task in front of everyone. By this stage of the day I was on a high, I had just passed what I could only describe as physically the hardest thing in my life by far and I wasn't going to fail now over a stupid knot. We all passed this part of the test and were congratulated. All that remained was to pass a medical examination and then a final interview; I floated back to Coventry that day. I had passed the physical and written tests – not bad for someone who was terrible at maths, scared of heights and slightly claustrophobic.

At the final interview one of the three officers who was conducting it asked me how I would feel if I was ever to see a dead body. To be honest, I didn't know as I had never seen a dead body. However, after passing all of the tests and getting this far I wasn't going to blow it now. 'Sir. I am sure I would be fine, no problem whatsoever.' He then replied, 'Well, never mind, some people never see a dead body throughout their whole career.'

I started at the fire service training school on April the 2nd 1990; it was a residential twelve-week course. The course was basically a continuation of the type of tests we had done to get into the fire service. It was a mixture of intense physical activity, on top of which we were bombarded with what felt like tons of academic information. We had to learn about the organisation, ranking structures, pumps, chemicals, gas, electricity, fire extinguishers and much more – it was constant pressure.

The days were very long, getting up at six o'clock in the morning to do our designated cleaning jobs, toilets, etc. and studying late into the night. I believed, and still do all of these years later, that we were bullied in training school. Some of the officers were great but there were at least two who should never have been put in charge of young recruits; to them it was a licence to bully and they certainly used it. A lot of the recruits had been in the armed forces and were used to this type of behaviour but to me it was a total shock. I didn't want to join the army; I wanted to be a firefighter.

This was a typical incident: I was up at 6 a.m. cleaning toilets, until an officer came and inspected my cleaning work. I cleaned everywhere – those toilets were gleaming – but I knew no matter how hard I tried he would always find something wrong. One day he put a pair of white cotton gloves on and rubbed his hand across the top of the door at the entrance to the toilet. He then looked at his fingers and with a big smile showed me a smudge mark on the glove. This meant that I had to write a report on why I had not cleaned the toilets properly and of course clean them again. This might not sound like a lot but the workload for the day was horrendous and the last thing I needed was to have to write a report on why some knob of an officer had decided to run a white glove over the top of a door that had probably never been cleaned since it had been there. These rituals were all about demeaning you and a chance for them to exert their powers and things like this happened several times a day, every day.

After our cleaning jobs they would take us out for long runs, sometimes even making us run through muddy ponds in a local park. We then had to do press-ups, sit-ups and whatever else they were in the mood for. Our kit had to be pristinely cleaned by the next day. Kit inspections were common place, a piece of fluff or a crease in the wrong place on a shirt leading to some form of punishment. This was day in, day out, from early morning to late at night, on top of tons of academic work and practical drills. It seemed relentless; one of the officers (a real knob) said that his aim was to break us down and rebuild us as new men and at times it felt like he was succeeding.

There were a few nights when I lay in my bunk bed and silently cried; although surrounded, I felt very alone. What had I done? I felt as though I would have been better off in the factory; at least there I was treated like an adult. This was horrible. I was married with two kids and I was being treated like a piece of shit and I didn't know if I could take it. I felt trapped and once again I felt like I didn't count, I was a nobody. This was a whole new world to me and I was not enjoying it one little bit. Once again I wanted to give in. I missed my family. I hadn't been bullied since I was at school, and at least there I could fight back. I wanted to flatten my antagonists, which would have been physically very easy for me to do. However, to do this would mean certain failure. How could I go home and face my family, knowing that I had given up? I knew that those old feelings of shame, disappointment and not being good enough were waiting to be reinforced. Some people did leave, it was too much for them, but I would not let those bullies win and I passed out from training school in the summer of 1990 with all of my family there to see my passing out parade. At long last I had achieved my dream. I was a very proud firefighter.

It had been a long three months of intense pressure at training school but I had survived. I had never realised just how much information my brain could take in or how far I could push myself physically but I had done it.

The main lesson that I learned through those difficult times was to keep going and not give in. So many times we are within touching distance of our goals but we succumb to outside pressures or our own fears. Sometimes even other people's fears can hold us back; for example, a wife or husband who may fear what effect you changing will have on them. As my good friend Geoff Thompson always says, get into the forge, stay there and mould yourself into whatever you want to become. The rewards for putting up with the heat of the forge are fantastic.

To be fair to the training school instructors, although I still think some of them were bullies, the standard of training was very good and this is vital in such a pressured job.

The first fire that I ever went to as a raw probationer was a person's reported incident. In fire service terms, this is a life or death incident; it means that someone is trapped in a burning building. I had heard so many stories from the older guys at the fire station about the risks they had taken at fires and all about the lives they had saved, as well as all the fatalities and near-death experiences they had experienced, so by the time it came to my first person's reported call I was terrified.

We set off from the fire station, blue lights flashing and sirens pounding out their shrilling cry. As it was a person's reported incident the driver went as fast as possible, weaving in and out of the traffic and crossing red traffic lights. In the back we were being tossed around like pancakes, bouncing all around the fire engine's cab whilst trying to put on our breathing apparatus.

As we arrived at the house we could see smoke and flames were pouring out of the upstairs windows. Concerned and panicked neighbours were telling us that a young mother lived there but that she had gone out and left her children at home alone.

I was partnering a more experienced firefighter. We quickly finished putting on our breathing apparatus and with charged hose reel in hand we entered the house. We headed for the stairs, our reasoning being that as it was night-time (about 10 p.m.) the children would most probably be in bed. I went to run up the stairs, as usual heart pounding and shaking like a leaf. My partner pulled me back and shouted, 'The stairs have gone.' In my eagerness to get to the kids I hadn't noticed that the middle of the stairs had been burned away. A ladder was quickly passed in to us and we placed this across the stairs and made our way up them and towards the fire.

I made my way into the first bedroom; I was on my hands and knees to stay below the smoke layer and using the light from the fire to search for bodies. I found a bed and felt all around and in it; at this point I couldn't see a thing. Unlike fires on programmes like *London's Burning* on television, in real fires, due to the thick, dense black smoke, visibility is virtually non-existent. My heart stopped as I felt a large lump in the bed. I pulled the lump towards me; it felt limp and lifeless. With baited breath I shined my torch onto what I presumed was its face. I found myself looking into the eyes of a big, furry stuffed tiger. I sighed with relief. I have never told a soul about the tiger as fire service humour is relentless and I would never have heard the end of it – 'Saved any stuffed toys recently, Tony?' We went on to put the fire out and thankfully there was nobody in the house.

This was my first real fire and what really surprised me about it was that because of time distortion, it all seemed to pass by like a blur. I now know in hindsight that when we are really scared the rational parts of our brains close down. So the theory in martial arts that the way you train is the way you will fight makes perfect sense. It was the same in the fire service; I was so scared during that incident that I wasn't thinking at all rationally. However, my training had been so good and so intense that when I looked back over the incident I had done everything in text-book fashion, which was fantastic.

The humour in the fire service is notoriously black, nothing is sacred. It starts off crude and gets even cruder. I often believed that this was a coping mechanism; sometimes we would see some horrific things. We never talked about feelings, sadness, fear, etc. so everything was turned into a joke. At least that way the incidents were discussed but through the guise of humour. I guess an outsider would be horrified at the thought of firefighters laughing at them but like I say, it was a good coping mechanism.

The humour was also directed at each other, the practical jokes being almost non-stop. These jokes ranged from filling someone's boots with water or eggs to turning people's personal lockers upside down and then back up the correct way, the idea being that they would return to find their locker looking perfectly normal from the outside, but when they opened it the contents would spill out and end up all over the locker room floor.

Once in a while someone managed to get hold of officially headed notepaper and we would organise for people to be transferred to other watches and even stations or to be sent on non-existent training courses. It was hilarious knowing that one of your colleagues was attending what he thought was his new station or watch only to be asked by the on-duty officer;

'Who the hell are you and what are you doing here?'
    'I'm your new watch member, sir.'
    'I think you've been had son, we don't have any new watch members.'

I know it might sound silly but trust me, at the time it was very funny. I did learn to be on constant guard in case I was the next victim.

New recruits always took some stick; I managed to avoid most of it as I was a bit older when I joined.

We arranged for one lad to go to bed in the middle of the day, telling him that this was to test if he could get to the fire engine in the allotted time if the alarms sounded. He climbed into his bed and we made sure he was nice and snug. As he waited for the alarms to sound someone went and told the officer in charge that the new lad had said he was feeling a bit tired and had gone to bed. The officer in charge was fuming and raced into the dormitory shouting and screaming;

'What the hell are you doing in bed?'
'But sir, it's the alarm test, sir.'
'I will give you a bloody alarm test, get out of that bed now!!'

Needless to say we were all rolling around laughing outside the door.

We told the same lad that it was his job to get up early in the morning at exactly 5.30 a.m. when we were on nights and bring the officer in charge a cup of tea. This particular officer in charge hated being woken up before 6.30 a.m., in fact, he just hated mornings and to put it mildly he could be very grumpy.

As good as gold, the young lad set his alarm and bang on 5.30 he knocked on the officer's door. It went something like this:
    Knock, knock (very gently).
    'WHAT?!'
    'Your tea, sir.'
    'WHAT FUCKING TEA? FUCK OFF!!'
    'Yes sir, very sorry sir, it won't happen again, sir.'
    'ARE YOU STILL THERE? I SAID FUCK OFF!'
    'Yes, sir.'

Another new recruit was told that it was his job to go on fire watch. This involved standing on the roof of Coventry's central fire station all night and watching out for any fires. After fits of laughter everyone else went to bed, leaving the poor young lad out doing his duty on a cold, wet roof. This trick did, however, backfire; the young lad spotted someone breaking into a shop in the city centre and called the police. He was a hero and had his picture on the front page of the local paper. Eagle-eyed Firefighter Catches Burglar. Although the papers never asked what he was doing standing on the roof of the fire station at 3 a.m. in the morning, a few senior officers did.

One of the best perks of being a firefighter was that when we were on duty on a Saturday night, on the way back from incidents we would often deliberately drive through the city centre to see groups of drunken women. The main reason for this was that quite often some attractive lady who'd had a few drinks would lift her top up and reveal her breasts, which obviously went down very well with the guys on the engine. We would be cheering and hoping for more while an enraged boyfriend tried to spoil the fun by covering her up.

However, this went awry one night in Wood End. We had a horrendously busy night – a big turf war was going on between two gangs. As part of this war the two gangs were petrol-bombing each other's cars and houses and we were caught in the middle. As we put a car fire out we were called straight away to a house fire in the next road and then back to the next car fire; it was exhausting. The main area of trouble seemed to be centred on one road. Every time we turned into this road we were met by the same group of people, who were a bit loud but never really gave us much trouble. The spokesperson for this group seemed to be a very large and loud woman. She had a can of cider in one hand and a fag in the other. Every second word out of her mouth seemed to be fuck: 'Fuck this, fuck that and fuck you.' As the night went on and her cider kicked in she seemed to get louder and louder and rougher and rougher, which was fine by us as we were far too busy to really care. However, she did overstep the boundary of decency when after about our seventh call to this particular road she decided to give us a treat by lifting up her top and showing us her bra.

What a difference a pair of boobs makes. We had gone from cheering at a glimpse of boob in the city centre to a mass groan in Wood End. Her bra must have been white at one time but had long since turned to a dirty off-grey colour, with large brown stains dotted all over it.

I thought Eddie beside me was going to throw up; it must have been the only time in my career as a firefighter that my colleagues and I hoped that someone would cover up a pair of breasts. To put it mildly, it wasn't a pretty sight.

I remained in the fire service for seventeen years and my great friend fear was a constant companion. I found myself in many frightening situations; in fact, I could and maybe will write a book on my experiences as a firefighter one day.

I never forgot the officer at my final interview who had asked me how I would feel if I ever saw a dead body, and then went on to tell me that I might never see one. In fact, throughout my career, I saw quite a lot of dead bodies and badly injured ones as well and although I always felt sad, I did cope.

I saw a baby who had been sleeping below a window into which a petrol bomb was thrown. Although it did not directly hit the baby we could see from her bright red face that she had been burned.

I saw another boy jump from a window after someone had set his parents' house on fire with a petrol bomb over an unpaid dept. The fire reached his bedroom, forcing him to jump. Once again he survived; he was lucky but he did get burned.

I saw people burned to death in house fires and in car crashes. When you see these things close up, when you see people fighting for their last breath, it makes you realise just how precious life truly is and it's a gift that we often take for granted.

Nobody sets out at the start of the day believing that they will die in a fire or a road traffic accident but it does happen. Sometimes these events are so random it is hard to believe how it actually happens.

We were called to an incident one night where a woman had offered to drive a colleague home from work. What's strange about that, you may ask. Normally this woman would not need a lift home but on this particular evening her car had broken down and coincidently on that night they both finished work at the same time (this did not usually happen). To complicate matters, this good Samaritan would normally be dropping someone else home but they were off work sick, so she felt obliged to drop her other colleague back at home after work. Coincidently, two young lads decided to steal a car that night. As they raced around in their stolen car they flew over the brow of a hill and collided with the woman's car, just as she was pulling out of the drive of the colleague she had just driven home. The two lads survived but she was killed almost instantly; on another night under other circumstances she would not have even been there.

Another woman driving to work in the early hours of the morning with hardly another car in sight at that ungodly hour noticed a car driving straight towards her on the wrong side of the road. At the last minute, just before they passed each other, the other car careered straight into her. The young lad driving the other car was very drunk, he had taken an overdose and had decided to kill himself by driving head on into an innocent driver coming in the other direction. When we arrived both cars were wrecked but he didn't have a scratch. She had internal injuries and was in a lot of pain but luckily her injuries were not life threatening.

Another incident we went to involved a young lad on a motorbike. Apparently he was going at a very fast speed up a residential road when a driver reversed his car out of his driveway and into the road. The motorbike was going so fast that he could not stop and he hit the car head on. When we arrived the motorcyclist, who was only a young lad, was lying motionless in the road. Two of us approached him to see what his injuries were and indeed if he had any. He looked perfect; apart from a small trickle of blood flowing from his nose there was not another mark on his body that we could see.

When we got close to him we knew straight away that he was not breathing; his perfectly intact looking body belied the fact that he had a broken neck. We carried out CPR but it was useless; he was gone.

Then there were the suicides, where people had set themselves on fire. What a horrific way to die. Any suspicious death always meant us hanging around for hours, normally somewhere near the burnt body while forensic teams investigated the death and took pictures for evidence in a coroner's court.

A typical example of scary situations that we experienced in the fire service was an incident I attended at a sixteen-storey block of flats in the red-light area of Coventry. Flat fires are a firefighter's nightmare: there is the obvious problem of getting water and resources up to the higher floors; the lifts can't be used, so getting to the flats can be difficult and space is greatly reduced in corridors. Early on in my career one of my West Midland colleagues based in Birmingham was killed in a flat fire. I always felt that flat fires had the greatest potential to go wrong and I was always on edge attending them. The procedures that are in place now have been greatly improved compared to what they were back then. To be honest, the procedures we did have, just as in this incident, were never really adhered to anyway.

When we got to this incident we were told that the fire was on the eight floor, so a firefighter called Pete Bentick, the officer in charge and I went up to the eight floor to have a look, whilst the crew members left behind started to get all the equipment ready that would be needed to fight the fire. When we got to the flat we were very surprised to see that the police were already there, talking to two young guys who apparently lived there. Pete and I put on our face masks and started up the oxygen on our breathing apparatus sets. We opened the door to the flat very carefully, not wanting to feed the fire with oxygen and make it worse. It was obvious to us because there was no big rush of heat or bellowing smoke that this wasn't an inferno but a slow-burning fire and if we got to it quickly we would be able to extinguish it before it could get any bigger.

I got hold of a hose reel from the landing of the flats; now this was considered to be a big no-no, as these hose reels were regarded as highly unreliable, often having been vandalised and having no water pressure. The right thing to do would have been to wait for the other members of our crew to bring the hose reel up from the fire engine to the fire. But this would have taken time and we were confident that this was a small fire so in we went with our little red hose reel in hand.

We crawled into the flat on our hands and knees, keeping below the layer of dense smoke. I was in front and Pete was pulling in the hose reel behind us. As we got further into the flat I could hear a strange noise. It's not unusual to hear strange things in fires, gushing water, exploding lights, etc. As I have already said, real fires are not like the ones you see on the television. In a real fire, visibility is virtually zero. An experienced firefighter may even delay putting the fire out, preferring instead to use the fire's visibility to look for any people or bodies that may be in the room. With such low visibility and lots of strange noises and sounds, fires can be very disorientating affairs.

I said to Pete, 'Can you hear that noise? What do you think it is?' He was as puzzled as I was. We kept going and eventually entered the kitchen. The noise was getting louder and louder. I noticed the glow of a small fire in what appeared to be a kitchen cupboard and we made our way over to it. As we got closer the noise got louder and louder, and to my horror I noticed that the fire was right next to a gas meter. To make this situation much worse, the supply pipe from the gas meter had been cut in half. The noise we could hear was the sound of gushing gas filling up the flat. For a split second (which seemed much longer) I froze. If the gas and air supply hit the correct mixture Pete and I would be blown to smithereens. The people standing outside the flat would be blown to smithereens. People in adjoining flats would be blown to smithereens. Any second now we could be dead. I wanted to get out of there, I wanted Pete to take charge. I was terrified but I knew I had to deal with this; how could I live with myself if I didn't? My heart was pounding, my stomach was in knots, I didn't know what to say to Pete and even if I had known what to say my mouth was so dry that I couldn't have said it anyway. At this point I noticed the key to turn off the gas supply was on the floor by the meter. I quickly picked it up, and I tried to put it on the valve that turns the meter off but my hands were shaking so much that I dropped it. Shit!! At a time like this the last thing I wanted to do was to drop the bloody key. I shakily picked it up again and this time managed to turn the gas supply off while Pete extinguished the fire.

Our job was done; we opened some windows to ventilate the flat (letting the smoke and gas out) and walked outside.

Outside the police had handcuffed the two young guys; apparently they had lit the fire deliberately. They thought it would be fun and that they would get a new flat. Pete turned to me, ashen-faced, and said, 'That was close, mate.' I smiled but I was just relieved to be alive. I thought of my kids and at that moment life again felt very precious. That incident was never mentioned again. Maybe Pete had felt as scared as me but in a job like the fire service it wouldn't do to admit that you were ever scared. It was a very macho environment and I never heard anyone admit to being scared. They were either all lying or I was the only frightened member of the whole of the bloody fire service!

Once again the dreaded fear feeling was brushed aside as if it had never happened but I knew it had definitely happened and so did Pete, even if we never admitted it to each other.

During my time in the service I saw many fatalities, which seemed to happen very randomly. We could go months without a fatality and then we would get two, three or even four together.

A few days before Christmas one year we went to an empty cargo aeroplane that had crashed just short of Coventry airport. The pilot had managed to avoid a large housing estate and crashed into a wooded area between the estate and the airport. We were the second crew to arrive and it was obvious straight away that no one had survived. After the initial fire had been extinguished I remember looking at some of the bodies protruding from the wreckage. The crew had consisted of five men.

Over the years I saw quite a few burnt bodies but they never looked real to me. I don't know if this was a coping mechanism on my part but I always thought of the bodies as mannequins and although this may sound a bit harsh, I never really felt any emotion for the person who had died. What I did feel, however, was a real sense of sadness for the relatives of those people who had died. For example, at the plane crash my first thoughts after the fire was out were that someone – a wife, daughter, son, mother – was going to be told that they had lost a son, dad or brother and that thought did fill me with sadness. I guess that for the rest of their lives Christmas would always have sad memories for them, being associated with the loss of a loved one.

I think the saddest thing I ever saw was at a road traffic accident where a young lad had driven a stolen motorbike through a crowd of young mothers and children as they came out of school. The handlebars of the bike hit a young mother in the stomach as she held her little boy's hand. At the same time the other side of the handlebars struck the little boy in the head. When we arrived there was pandemonium, children were crying, parents were screaming. The young lad who had been riding the motorbike was lying on the floor a few feet away from the boy and his mother.

I would guess that the little boy was aged around five or six years of age. The boy and his mother were virtually motionless and very quiet but the motorcyclist was screaming in agony; it turned out that he had broken his ankle in the collision. A member of our crew was sent to give him first aid, while myself and the others stayed with the little boy and his mother. The little boy's body was shaking but he never made a sound, he just lay on his back, glazed eyes wide open, staring at the sky; it was a horrible sight to see. His mum was in obvious pain – she had suffered internal injuries, which we found out later included broken ribs and a ruptured spleen. She moaned in agony but kept reaching her hand out in a blind search for her child and murmuring, 'I want my baby, I want my baby.' A young firefighter held the little boy's hand; I will never forget this picture for as long as I live. As he held his little hand a trickle of wee left his young, fragile and beautiful body, weaving its way around the firefighter's glove and into the gutter.

The paramedics were very quickly on the scene and as usual they were brilliant. A doctor also arrived; the paramedics were going through their procedures on the boy when the doctor stopped them. One of the paramedics questioned him, not in a negative way, but still questioned him. The doctor's reply has always stayed with me, 'Listen to what the patient is telling us', which I took to mean, I know that you have your procedures but his bodily reactions are dictating that we do things differently this time and I loved that. To me that was confidence in his ability as a doctor, to know the rules and yet to be able to break them if the circumstances dictated that he should.

I never felt that I ever suffered from post-traumatic stress but for a few weeks after that incident even if I was out shopping, whenever I saw a small boy with his mother, especially if they were holding hands, I would see the face of the little boy lying in the road and this really upset and disturbed me but I never told anyone and just carried on with my life. I never did learn what happened to the boy, his mother or the lad on the motorbike. That's just the way it was at that time in the fire service, we just got on with our job, no questions asked. No one asked me or any of the other guys if we were traumatised and to be honest, if they had done so I would have never admitted to my feelings. To do so would have felt like admitting a weakness and I was now a man's man, I was tough and brave, at least on the outside.

I was in the fire service for seventeen years and had some great experiences and met some fantastic people. I was always very proud of myself for passing the rigorous entrance tests and I was very proud to be a member of the West Midlands fire service.

However, with the advent of public service cuts, subsequent strikes and business plans being introduced to the service, the role of firefighter changed dramatically; to me, it seemed to change from being a vocation to being just another job, and morale was at rock bottom. I found this hard to take and was becoming bored with all of the new working practices. Anyone who complained was quickly told, 'Well, you know where the door is if you don't like it, there are thousands of people out there who would love to have your job.' I listened to my colleagues moaning every day about how bad the job had become and how good it had been in the good old days.

All of this moaning reminded me of my time in the car factory and so I knew it was time to move on. I could stay in the job for my remaining ten years, moan along with the others, collect my pension and leave (99 % of people chose this option) or I could leave now. One guy was moaning about the job so much one night that I said to him, 'Have you ever thought about leaving?' He put both of his hands towards me as if they were handcuffed together and said, 'Golden handcuffs, mate.' In doing this he was referring to his pension, which was still at least fifteen years away. He knew and I knew that there was nothing tying his hands together; the handcuffs were just imaginary and gave him an excuse not to face his fears and risk change. In careers like the fire service and other public sector jobs, pensions are used as the number one excuse as to why people can't leave.

I completely understand this but why work in misery year after year for something that you might not even live to see anyway? Why waste your life away doing a job that you no longer like?

I have always thought that we should be enjoying life, not just surviving it. I heard some people use the pension excuse even though they had only been in the job for a few very short years. People moaned like merry hell about the job but then would say, 'If it wasn't for my pension, I would leave.' But I knew that just as in the case of those people in the car factory who said, 'If only I had my time again, things would be different,' this just wasn't true; fear was keeping them there, and they knew it, too.

I chose to leave but only after a lot of very painful soul searching; this was one of the scariest decisions I had ever made. I also had many false starts. I would go into work telling myself that today was the day I would hand my notice in, only to come up with an excuse as to why I shouldn't do it. Being honest, it probably took me about a year to finally hand in my notice and even then I said I would take a career break for a year rather than sever all my ties straight away (this was a bit of a safety net in case my new career didn't take off).

The night before I handed in my notice I told Beverley my plans. She had heard it all before and just said, 'OK, Anthony, whatever makes you happy.' I got the distinct impression from her tone that she didn't believe I was finally going to do it. But this time I did mean it. I went into work the next day and told my boss, station officer Paul Saddler, I was leaving. Paul was one of the better officers I had served under and he just said, 'Look, just think about your decision, Tony, and make sure you are doing the right thing.' I told him I had been thinking about it for a long time, that I didn't know if it was the right thing to do or not, only that I had to do it. I then went and told the rest of my watch that I would be leaving. I think they secretly admired me but still came out with the old lines: 'What about your pension?' 'How will you survive without any money?' They even kindly offered to send me food parcels at Christmas if I was starving. They were a good bunch and leaving them would be very hard.

I handed in my notice and said that I would leave just after Christmas; I wanted to make sure Christmas was a good one before I jumped into what was looking like a very uncertain future. Over the previous three years I had been successfully studying to become a counsellor and I now had a couple of counselling clients. I also had half a dozen or so self-defence clients but I knew that I would have to get substantially more work than this if I was going to make my future plans work.

As the time got closer to leaving, I would find myself waking up in the middle of the night once again, sweating and my heart pounding; this was a slow release of my old friend adrenalin. I was facing an uncertain future and I was scared, Beverley wasn't best pleased with me and I understood her concerns as well. What if everyone was right? What if I couldn't make this work? What if I couldn't pay my bills? What if I lost everything, including my wife? What about my pension? What if I had to go back cap in hand to the fire service for my old job back? What if they wouldn't give it back to me? What if they all laughed at me? Those old feelings of shame, disappointment and failure were once again hovering over my head, just waiting to pounce and be reaffirmed. It felt as though I was torturing myself. I also noticed, perhaps in hindsight, that all the questions I was asking myself were well and truly based in the negative side of my brain. Knowing what I know now, I would reframe all of those questions and, for example, say, what if things do work out? What if you are a success? What if people don't laugh at you but admire you?

I had been a firefighter for seventeen years. It had been my dream job and now I was leaving.

If I was to say that I was scared, it would be the understatement of the century – I was terrified. I was approaching what I would call the terror barrier and I was beginning to see how it had got that name.

On my last ever shift in the West Midlands fire service I handed all of my uniform and the keys to my locker over to Dave Curry, who was a leading firefighter on my watch. This was it, I was really leaving, and I felt sad, scared, empowered, relieved, excited and apprehensive all at the same time. I felt as though I was leaving a big part of myself behind but I knew that it was an old part. I knew that if I wanted to grow as a person that I would, metaphorically speaking, have to shed my old skin and the fire service was a very big part of that skin. I knew then and it is even clearer to me now that nothing stays the same; the fire service, me and you are continually moving forward in a never-ending cycle of birth and death. Our bodies are dying and being reborn all of the time, this process never ends. Are you still the same person that you were ten years ago? Or even twenty years ago? Or are those just old parts of you that are gone forever, only returning now and then as distant memories?

These old parts cling on to us for dear life, they are our identities We have normally taken years to form these identities so it is no wonder that we struggle to let them go.

For seventeen years I had been Anthony the firefighter and now the question was, who am I? What or who was I to become? The fire service was a given, a known, security, and I was now stepping into the unknown. I have heard it said that freedom and security are at the opposite ends of life's scales. It can be said that prisoners are the most secure people in our society, with all of their basic needs being met by the system – warmth, food, shelter, etc. They pay the price for these basic needs by sacrificing their freedom. The first couple of weeks after leaving the fire service felt like a honeymoon period. I was adapting to life without putting out fires or getting up for work. Then I started to think about bills and earning money. Beverley was very supportive but then again she always had been; however, I knew that she was worried about our financial situation. I had never been the type of person to plan things and I was being true to form – I didn't really have a plan now. I started to worry about where the money was going to come from and a sense of panic started to sink in. I had half expected this to happen but not this early in my new adventure.

Three good friends of mine had encouraged me to take the leap of faith and leave the fire service.

Geoff Thompson, who I consider to be a great friend and mentor to me, had left his factory job many years ago. He went on to become an internationally renowned martial artist and writer of many self-defence and motivational books. He even won a BAFTA for a short script he wrote for a film which starred Ray Winstone.

Then there was Glen Smith, another very good friend of mine. Glen had been a scaffolder and left this to teach one-to-one boxing sessions at a local gym. He was so successful that he eventually opened his own gym, which is called the Red Corner gym in Coventry. Glen and the gym are amazing. I teach there and along with everyone else who goes there I love it.

The third person who I classed as a very good friend was Paul Browning; Paul had been a sergeant in the West Midlands police force for eleven years. I met Paul through my martial arts training; he actually came to me for self-defence lessons, which was ironic as he was a self-defence instructor in the police. We became good friends and have helped each other through some troublesome times. Paul now runs his own IT company and is very successful.

Although I classed these three people as very good friends, now that times were starting to get a little bit rough (financially) I started to curse them. They had all encouraged me to take the leap and leave my job but where were they now? Why had I listened to them? It was all right for them, they had made it – but what about me? I felt alone, abandoned. What had I done to deserve this?

After feeling sorry for myself for a few days I realised that I had to take responsibility for my own actions; no one had made me do anything, it was all my own decision. I looked at my situation. One of the things I had learned to do over recent years was to take a step back and look at myself. What was I focusing on? I know that what we focus on gets bigger and can become our reality. Your perception is your reality; you create your own world, or at least your own version of it. I soon realised that I had been focusing on having no money and this was exactly what I was getting. I changed my focus and kept telling myself everything was going to be OK, soon the money would start rolling in. Over the next couple of days my phone was very busy. People were calling me to book self-defence lessons and I was getting more and more counselling work. Once again I was getting what I was focusing on, only this time it was making more money, the lesson here being that what you focus on you will get, so be very careful what you ask for and focus your attention on because you might just get it.

I believe that risk is a big part of life, or at least it should be. Taking risks can be scary but if we never take those risks then how can we change? I have taken many risks and every time I have taken a risk I have had big helpings of fear as a companion, gently whispering in my ear, 'Don't do it, you will fail, stick with what you have now.' All I can say is that I am still alive and I am enjoying my life.

If the great teachers, scientists and explorers of the past had never taken risks then our world would be a very different place today.

John Verti SJ puts this much better than me:

To love is to risk not being loved in return.
To live is to risk dying.
To hope is to risk despair.
To try is to risk failure.
But risk must be taken, because the greatest hazard in life is to risk nothing.
The person who risks nothing has nothing. They may avoid suffering and sorrow but they simply

cannot learn, feel, change, grow love and live. Chained by their fortitudes, they are a slave, they have forfeited freedom.

Only a person who risks is free.

Teach me to listen to those nearest to me, make me aware of the message, accept the person I am, listen to me.

Teach me to listen to those far from me. The plea of the forgotten, the cry of the anguished.

Teach me to listen to myself. Help me to be less afraid, to trust the voice inside, in the deepest part of me.

THE HEALER

By now you may have realised that as well as being a risk taker, I am stubborn, determined and full of fear but also a rescuer. I derive a great deal of pleasure from helping other people. Having carried out a great deal of self-analysis I now realise that we all need to feel significant. One of the ways I get to feel significant is by helping or rescuing other people, which is perfectly OK as long as I realise that this is about me and my needs.

If I am not careful, it can be a bit like seeing a blind man waiting at the side of a busy road and helping him to cross. You might think, what's the problem with that? The problem is that in this case the blind man did not even want to cross the road, he was perfectly happy where he was, he did not ask for help.

Life is full of games and these games are going on everywhere. Games at work, games in families and games in relationships – you can be involved in various games at the same time and in lots of different areas of your life. Games are perfectly OK as long as you know the rules. Sometimes, for example in relationships, people change and make up the rules as they go, which can be very frustrating, a bit like moving the goalposts when you are just about to score a goal.

Most of the time people do not even realise that they are in a game. If you can see the games being played then you have a choice; either play along and obey the rules or make up your own rules to suit your own needs. It is my experience that people do take on a role; whether you like it or not you will be playing many different roles in many different situations. Are you different at work to how you are at home?

Even in families it is not unusual, for example, for one parent to take on the role of the good guy, leaving the other parent in the role of the bad guy.

In my search for significance and my subsequent need to help everybody I meet, if I am not careful I can cause more harm than good.

I have never liked bullies and would often race to the aid of a bully's victim, which could and often did lead to confrontation for me. I just could not stand by and watch a human being pick on another helpless human being. I have never liked injustice, as I perceive it, either on an individual basis or even an international basis (for example, a big country attacking a smaller country, but let's not get into the minefield of politics!).

As a firefighter, one of the obvious perks of the job as far as I was concerned was that I got to rescue people. Imagine my reaction as a rescuer when the fire service asked for volunteers to become fire setter tutors. A fire setter tutor was someone who visited children aged up to sixteen who had been in trouble, usually with the police, for lighting fires. The government had commissioned some research which had asked long-term prisoners how they had started a life of crime in the first place. Most of them said that they had started with small crimes like arson or petty thieving but that there had been no one to show them the error of their ways, no role models. So the idea was to send out trained firefighters to talk to these children as soon as they started getting into trouble and to hopefully steer them onto the right path. This idea appealed to me (as a rescuer). Being brought up on a rough council estate, I had witnessed many of my friends get into trouble and eventually end up in prison.

One of the biggest thieves on the estate who had been in every institute for offenders known to man once told me about the first time he was sent to a detention centre. When the judge passed sentence and said he was going to be locked away, he felt a wave of emotion flow through his body. His eyes filled with tears as he searched the courtroom in a vain attempt to be rescued. He saw his dad and through tear-filled eyes said, 'Dad, please help me, please dad, please don't let them take me away.' His dad just said coldly, 'You will be OK, son,' turned his back and nonchalantly walked out of the courtroom. My friend said that he had never felt so alone and realised at that moment in time that his dad just didn't care, in fact nobody cared. That simple act of his dad turning his back said so much and led to intense feelings of anger, rage, rejection, sadness, hurt and even devastation as well as a life full of crime.

I have seen many cases like this. I knew that most of these kids were not bad people, they just needed some guidance which was all too often missing in their lives. I honestly felt that if I could talk to some of these young fire lighters, as we jokingly called them, then I could help them turn away from a life of crime and misery. So I volunteered to become a fire setter tutor.

This decision was to have a dramatic effect on my life. Before I was set free on members of the public I had to attend a two-day course in basic counselling skills. I absolutely loved the course; we talked about listening skills, empathy, the ego and other fascinating areas. At the end of the two days we were all told, 'You are trained counsellors now, so off you go and counsel.' I very quickly found myself out of my depth. The kids were fine but more often than not it was the parents who needed counselling, especially the mums. The mums would often be heartbroken; they could see the paths that their children were on and they didn't like it one little bit. They often felt alone, helpless and powerless to do anything, so as soon as they had someone to listen to them, they would let it all out. I went back to my employers and told them of my concerns. Their answer was to send me on an advanced two-day counselling course, which was once again great but not very in depth.

Although I had only covered the very basics in counselling skills I was hooked; this whole area and way of working with people just felt so right. I wanted to learn more so I contacted my local colleges to find out what courses they were running in coaching or counselling. Tile Hill College in Coventry had been running counselling courses for many years and were about to start a new certificate course in humanistic counselling. People often ask me, 'How did you choose what type of counselling to study?' To be honest, I didn't do any research whatsoever but just chose what was on offer. I didn't know the difference between the various counselling approaches (there are lots of different types of therapy) and back then I didn't really care.

The course I actually attended was held in very high regard in the counselling world. The tutors were all top class and excellent teachers and as it turned out, because of local politics, it would be the last course that they ever ran. All of this was unbeknown to me at the time. I guess I was just lucky, that's if you believe in luck; I believe I was being guided towards the best people by my ever faithful guardian angel. So that's how my journey into the amazing world of counselling began and what a journey it has turned out to be.

Breaking into the world of counselling was as scary to me as any of the physical confrontations I had experienced. For example, due to an administration error, I started the certificate course (which was a one-year course consisting of attending college one evening per week) a week later than everyone else. I turned up at Tile Hill College in Coventry on a Monday evening, only to be told when I found my classroom that my classmates were all getting to know each other and I was to just walk in and say hello to everyone.

I had not been in any education for a long time and what's more, when I had been, to put it mildly, I hadn't actually excelled. At this point I had a picture of my fellow students all being teachers or social workers and being very clever academically. So here I was, being expected to walk into a classroom full of people who would be much more intelligent than me and say, 'Hello everyone, my name is Tony.'

I felt like an idiot just thinking about having to do this, let alone actually doing it.

At this point the negative little voice in my head said, 'Why don't you just turn around and go home, save yourself all of this undoubted embarrassment? You're not going to fit in here, these people are far too intelligent for you. What makes you think a kid from Wood End could ever become a counsellor?' Once again, just as I had done many times in the past, I stepped forward, turned the handle and stepped right into my fears and just like every other time I was terrified.

After I had said a rather uncomfortable hello to a few people we were all invited to sit down. The tutor, Jim Murphy, then asked us to write one major fear we had about the course on a piece of paper and then fold it up and place it on the floor in the middle of the room. I wrote that I was worried that I wouldn't be able to keep up academically with the rest of the class. I sat back and viewed my fellow students; I was one of only two men in a class of twenty people. The other guy looked like a university professor, the other people in the room did indeed look like teachers and social workers.

I had heard that most counsellors were middle-aged, middle-class women and this group certainly seemed to reflect that theory. One by one we were all invited to pick a piece of paper from the centre of the room; no one knew what anyone else had written. Then, one by one, people read out what was written on the piece of paper they had chosen. I could not believe my own ears, people were saying things like, 'I am scared I won't fit in', 'I am scared I won't be clever enough, what if the class reject me?' This continued for the next twenty minutes. I tried to look calm but my gaze was darting around the room trying to work out who had written what but this was an impossible task.

I was amazed. Everyone in that room, no matter what their background was, had a fear and most of it was about fitting in and being accepted by the rest of the class; we were all scared. Yet again I wasn't alone with my fears, and to know this was very comforting. I felt the depressive weight of fear that I had placed around my own shoulders once again start to lighten.

The certificate course took a year to complete and in that year I got to know and like my fellow students. They were all nice people who just wanted to better themselves and to help others to do the same.

The next step was to do a diploma in counselling which followed on from the certificate; the diploma would take two years to complete and would mean attending college one day a week for two years. Because of the shifts I was working in the fire service I had struggled at times to attend one evening a week for the certificate course, so how on earth was I going to be able to attend one day a week for the next two years?

The fire service had been very good in helping me with the costs of the course. I had put forward a good case that my counselling skills would help me in my relationships with my work colleagues and also distressed members of the public and of course my fire setter tutoring. After hearing my argument they agreed to meet half the costs of the course.

The diploma alone would cost £3,000, which was a lot of money to me. However, they would not give me any time off work to attend the course. I needed a plan. To pay the other half of the course I decided to convert my garage into a gym and teach grappling and self-defence lessons. The garage was freezing and had no lights but with a little forethought and an extension lead running from my kitchen window I made it work. I told my clients in the winter that the cold was good for physical conditioning and was good character building material; they seemed to like this idea.

As for getting the time off work, I decided to use my holidays and take all of my overtime as time off in lieu instead of money and if need be I would work Saturday nights for people on other shifts in exchange for a Tuesday daytime. I had no shortage of takers on this deal.

Sometimes after completing a night shift, I would go straight to college for the day and then go back to work that night for my next shift. But once again I was determined to complete the course and qualify as a counsellor and nothing was going to stop me.

Part of the criteria for passing the diploma was that all students had to do one hundred hours of actual hands-on counselling. This would mean getting a placement with a counselling agency and we were told that this was not always easy as counselling was starting to get quite popular and there were more counsellors than there were jobs.

I applied to various counselling agencies without much success, that is until I contacted Hinckley Mind and was asked to go for an interview. I attended the interview and was offered a placement as a counsellor, which was great news.

As I walked away from the interview I was over the moon but then a thought hit me; Mind was an organisation that dealt with people who had mental health problems, what did I know about mental health? What was I letting myself in for? All I had cared about was getting a placement to meet the criteria of my course, I didn't really care where that placement was or the type of clients I would be working with.

To be completely honest, I was very naïve in my attitude to the whole area of mental health. One of my favourite films of all time was *One Flew Over the Cuckoo's Nest*, starring Jack Nicholson. I would be working with a load of nutters, how the hell was I going to counsel a nutter?

I have to say that my two years as a voluntary counsellor at Hinckley Mind were fantastic. The people who worked there were so nice and supportive, as were the clients. I met some great people and my views towards the whole area of mental health have completely changed. It is a much misunderstood field and without a doubt a much neglected area of care. Most of the clients I saw there were suffering from different levels of depression – some had compulsive disorders, and some had suffered a relationship breakdown or bereavement.

Mental illness is just like any other illness, in that people can and thankfully often do recover. However, where it differs from other illnesses is that it has a horrible stigma attached to it and once people are labelled it can be very hard to get rid of that label. These were just normal people who were going through a very hard time and fortunately there are agencies like Mind out there to help them through.

I saw lots of clients during my time at Mind. A few really stand out in my memory. There was the business lady who used to come and see me on her lunch break from work. She was always dressed very smartly in a black suit and white blouse and had immaculate make-up. She would talk about her family problems and her relationship with her new partner.

One day I noticed that whenever we talked about her work she would sit and constantly tap her foot. When I asked her about this her face changed from white to pink, and for a few seconds there was silence. When she eventually spoke she said that she worked in an office and she was the only woman in her team. It was her job to sort out any problems the rest of the team had with their work. She would sit at her desk trying to look calm as these men talked about their problems. It was her job to find solutions. She wanted to give off an air of confidence but underneath she felt very uncomfortable and she was full of self-doubt. What if she didn't know the answers? What would they think about her? Would they think she was stupid? Above the desk she was calm and in control but below the desk her foot was tapping like mad. She was terrified that they would all see she wasn't as good as she was portraying herself to be.

This story reminded me of a swan gliding gracefully across a lake; what you don't see are its little legs paddling like mad under the surface. This lady's fear was that if these men saw any weakness in her then they would laugh at her and, even worse, reject her. What I have learned is that our perceived weaknesses can often be our strengths. We all feel vulnerable and have self-doubts but while we ignore these doubts they get bigger and bigger. They certainly don't go away but by getting them out into the open we expose them for what they really are, which is illusions created by our own minds. Our minds are powerful enough to create a picture, which is an illusion. But then by adding feelings and endless thoughts we can make that illusion into a real thing. How powerful is that? We are all capable of picturing something in our own minds and then of bringing that picture to life. A word of warning: be very careful what illusions you pay attention to because there is a good chance that you will soon be living in them and they will become your reality.

When we expose our own doubts we encourage and allow others to do the same. Yes, she may have been taking a risk in exposing her fears but my guess is that the people in her office, who undoubtedly would have their own self-doubts and fears, would have admired her for doing this, and so her weakness would then become her strength.

There is a time to be guarded but it is also important to know when it is safe enough to lower our guards. Also, by trying to hide her self-doubt she was making her working life very uncomfortable – it was taking a lot of effort to keep the mask of pretence raised in a vain effort to stop people seeing what I guess they already knew anyway.

One of my favourite sayings in the Bible is 'to thine own self be true'. I have met so many people throughout my life, as I am sure you have, who pretend to be something they are not. Take the guy who continually brags about his achievements in a vain attempt to impress his friends – all he ends up doing is alienating the very people who he so desperately wants to accept him; they run when they see him coming. If only he could drop the pretence, the need to impress, his friends would probably accept him a lot more easily. But that would involve taking a risk and saying, 'You know what, I don't have all the answers and I do get scared and worried about certain things. This is me, this is who I am and this is what I believe.'

My guess is that for most of us, when we have revealed our perceived weaknesses in the past we may have been ridiculed or laughed at and that prevents us from being true to ourselves in the present moment. We don't want to risk that feeling of being hurt again, it can be very painful.

That feeling of hurt comes from the feeling of being rejected by those we look to for love and support. What I have realised is that the only person who can reject you is you. In our efforts to fend off this perceived rejection we create identities or masks to hide behind. These defence mechanisms are fine for a time and do serve a real purpose. The problem arises when we realise that we are not being true to our real inner selves. We start to fear that our masks will slip and people will see what is hidden behind them and then we will certainly face ridicule and rejection. Sometimes these defences or masks just get too heavy; they no longer serve a purpose. We feel the urge to let them go; however, because we have held on to them for so long this can be a very scary process. It is my belief that many of us will go through our whole lives hiding behind these masks or identities, too scared to let them slip, and because of this we never reveal our true selves. As the saying goes, we die with our best song still in us, too scared to sing, too scared to be heard or seen, and this is very sad. The real you is never revealed and all because of what someone else might think or say.

It is my belief that the real you, hidden behind all of those layers of past conditioning, is God. Underneath all of those layers, hidden away is the most powerful energy source in the whole universe. The part of us that we are scared to reveal is powerful beyond belief.

We give other people tremendous power over us by caring too much about what they may think or say. We tend to compare ourselves to others and very often in our own minds we come up short in comparison.

Another person I remember very clearly from my time at Mind was a middle-aged man who said he was suffering from depression. He felt as though his life was falling apart. He had lost his job as a delivery driver which he had held for over twenty years. He had turned to alcohol for comfort and a way out of his misery; this in turn had the knock-on effect of him neglecting his family and his wife finding solace in the arms of another man.

My client was a husband and father. He had been the breadwinner and role model in his family for the last twenty years but now he felt with the loss of his job that all of this had been taken away from him. One day he said, 'Tony, everyone thinks I am a great guy, the nicest guy in the pub. I have a laugh and a few drinks but on the inside I feel like a little insignificant worm about this big.' He held out his shaky hand with his thumb and finger about an inch apart, and tears rolled down his cheeks. This guy had built up an image of being a big, tough, strong man but once this image was threatened, in this instance with the loss of his job, his image, or as I like to call it his mask, came tumbling down and underneath was the worm. The foundations of his whole being were built on sand, as are so many other people's, especially men. We all feel vulnerable at times but for many men to admit this would be unthinkable because they have put so much time and effort in to creating this tough persona or identity. Once again I guess his fear was that if he told his wife and son how he was feeling that they would reject him and not see him as a man anymore, when in reality his denial and turning to drink had forced them to turn away and abandon him anyway. The very thing that he did not want to happen was happening and he felt as though there was nothing he could do about it. Maybe if he had admitted how he was really feeling his family would have rallied around him and helped him through those difficult times, whereas hitting the bottle had only amplified his problems.

The weaker we feel on the inside the stronger the defences we try to build on the outside. Every time I turn on the news and hear various people talking about how much our armed forces cost to maintain it always reminds me of the forces we use to protect our self-image and perceived vulnerabilities.

Maintaining these defences can be very costly, only the cost to the individual is usually a lot more than just financial. It's also very important to remember it's not what has happened to us in the past that really counts; it is how we interpret what has happened that is really important. It's even more important that we learn from our past experiences and use this learning to shape our future. You can dwell on the past or move forward with your hard-earned experiences and shape a brighter future.

After working at Mind for two years I decided that it was time to broaden my counselling skills and move on. I heard through the counselling grapevine that Myton Hospice was looking for volunteer counsellors. I wanted to be the best counsellor that I could possibly become and past experience had shown me that to do this I would have to work in the hardest of areas.

The thought of working in a hospice filled me with trepidation, Could I work with people who were dying? Could I work with the relatives of those who had died? The fact that it was so scary told me that this was the direction I should take, so I applied for the role of voluntary counsellor at Myton Hospice.

As soon as I walked into the hospice grounds I knew that I was in a very special place. It was so peaceful, tranquil and it had an overall feeling that I find very hard to put into words; the only word that comes close to describing this feeling is spiritual.

I am a big believer in energy; in fact, I truly believe that you, me and everything in this universe are made of the same energy. God, who I believe is pure love, is also energy; in God's case, love energy.

We have all experienced people in our lives who seem to drain our energy (energy Hoovers), while other people seem to have the ability to re-energise us. Myton Hospice was overflowing with energy, it was an amazing place.

By this time I had finished my diploma and was a qualified counsellor but even so, before I could work at the hospice I would have to attend one of their complicated bereavement courses.

On this course all of the participants were asked to think about their own deaths. What would your funeral be like? Who would be there? What would they say about you? What regrets would you have about your life? What songs would you choose to have played? If you knew you only had a short time left to live, what would you do differently? A good question to ask yourself at this point is, if knowing what I know now, I was given the chance to live my life all over again, what would I do differently? You can apply this question to any area of your life: work, relationships and so on. I highly recommend that you do this little exercise now, remembering that it's not too late to change.

Another thought-provoking question to ask yourself is, if I could be the perfect person, what would I look like and be like? What traits or characteristics would your ideal person have? My guess is that when you do this exercise you will find that you already have a lot of these traits; you are already close to being your ideal person. If you are not, then you now know which areas of your character and life you have to work on.

I guess to some people this may sound like a morbid exercise but I believe that it is a very important thing to do. We would be working with death and the dying, possibly on a daily basis. After all, we are all dying, it's something that we often don't like to think about but it's one of life's certainties. Ghandi said he was dying and being reborn every day.

The cycle of birth and death cannot be denied but by facing it we can make it less daunting and more acceptable. By looking at my own death and bringing it into my reality I was left with the feeling that my life is precious, it will end but I want to enjoy every second of it that I have left. By the same token, everyone around me is precious and I want to value and enjoy their lives as well. Everything around us is going to end, enjoy it while you can and like the old song says, 'enjoy yourself, it's later than you think'.

Counselling at the hospice was very different to counselling at Mind; sometimes I saw people on the wards, sometimes they would be just too ill to see.

All counselling is based around good listening skills, which most people think that they have, but in reality very few people are good listeners. It's worth noting at this point that most of us have two ears and one mouth, so it would be worth using them in this ratio and not, as is often the case, the other way round. When working with someone who has lost a very close member of their family, for example a child, these listening skills are vital. It is often the case that there is nothing that anyone can say or do to make these people feel any better but what we can do is to be there for them and support them in their greatest time of need.

Once again, just as I had done at Mind, I found that my knowledge of hospice work was bordering on being ignorant. I thought that people went to a hospice to die but this is not always the case; people often go to hospices for help with pain relief or to visit drop-in centres where they can see and mix with other sufferers. Because they are run on charitable donations there tends to be more demand than actual places at the hospices and often people have to be refused a place.

The care given from the staff was amazing; a lot of the doctors and nurses had left the NHS because they felt that they didn't have time to spend with the patients. In my view, the NHS is a fantastic organisation but sadly, like most public services, it is starting to be run like a business and as such there are far too many restraints placed on the staff, especially time restraints. In hospices the atmosphere is much more relaxed and the staff do have the time to sit with their patients and their families and explain everything that is happening (good old-fashioned patient care).

As a counsellor I worked with people who were dying or people whose relatives had died at the hospice. In the case of bereavement this could often be long-term work; most people started to feel a little bit better after a year. This makes sense because in that first year they have to cope with lots of anniversaries and painful reminders of what they have lost – birthdays, Christmas, wedding anniversaries and many more. Because many of the cases were long term and I was only working there part time on a voluntary basis (I was still in the fire service), I never really saw that many clients.

One of those clients was a lovely lady who was dying from cancer and actually passed away a few months after I started working with her, which was very sad. Another lady I worked with had watched her daughter pass away at the hospice; this once again was very sad and my hardest times as a counsellor have been without a doubt working with parents who have lost a child.

I do believe we should embrace death as it is indeed a certainty but this is easier to do if things are in the correct order. For a parent to bury a child is totally devastating and certainly not in the correct order of things. My heart goes out to anyone who has been through this experience and all I can say is that hopefully one day it will all make sense in God's greater scheme of things. I like the theory that life doesn't just begin at birth and end at death. I also like the theory that before we are born, we are souls waiting to come to earth. Some of these souls know that they will be here for a long time and some for a short time. We all go back to the same place.

I also worked with a man whose wife had died, leaving him with two small children. As well as being heartbroken he was also very angry, which is not unusual in cases of bereavement. There are many stages of bereavement and these can be different for different people.

As a counsellor my job was to help my clients accept the reality of their loss and work through the pain of grief, then adjust to an environment where the deceased is missing, and finally come to terms with it and move on with life.

These feelings or stages often apply when relationships break up, as loss is the general theme and it can have a traumatic effect on all of us.

I went into the hospice as someone who was very nervous around death and people who were actually dying. What would I be able to say to them? What could I say to make them feel better? Would I be of any help to them at all?

I left the hospice after two years with a completely different outlook on death; I believe it has made me appreciate my life even more by acknowledging that it is going to end. I want to make the most of it and I am sure that if those people who have gone to the next world before us could give us any advice it would be along the lines of enjoy it all, live every minute and love everyone and everything. I am also in awe of the people who work in hospices; every news bulletin in a paper or on television is full of negativity but we never hear about the people who devote their lives to caring for others. For every negative piece of news in the world there are ten positive acts that don't get reported but they are happening right now as you read this book.

Once again, listening to some of the stories of things that happen in hospices I found myself in awe of the human mind. It is not unheard of for people to put off their own deaths until they have seen a certain loved one – how powerful is that? We can even choose our exact time of death. We come into the world at just the right time and we leave it at just the right time, too.

After leaving the hospice I continued to develop my counselling skills. I studied NLP up to master practitioner level, which included time line therapy and hypnotherapy. I viewed counselling like martial arts and tried to study as many different styles as I could, taking the best that they all had to offer. I heard people in the counselling world knock NLP and I heard far more life coaches and NLP practitioners knock counselling but I refused to be swayed and studied them all, believing that they all would have something to offer.

One of the things I have found worrying about the coaching arena is the amount of people calling themselves life coaches. A lot of these people have no real qualifications or just a few basic ones that are not worth much. To qualify as a counsellor I had to go through my own personal therapy and do one hundred hours on a placement over three years. Compare this to someone who has done a one-week NLP course or a basic hypnotherapy course and then start calling themselves life coach consultants.

I am quite sure that these people find themselves out of their depth very quickly but what damage do they cause in the meantime?

I was still working as a firefighter at this stage and on my days off I would teach self-defence lessons at the Red Corner gym in Coventry. I also hired a room by Coventry train station and was seeing one or two private counselling clients a week. Glen Smith, who ran the gym, asked me if I would see a young boxer at the gym called Troy James. Glen said Troy was showing a lot of potential but for some reason (Glen thought this was psychological) he was losing the occasional fight.

I agreed to see Troy, who informed me that he was getting a lot of chest infections, which was affecting his training, and that his doctor had arranged for him to go to a local hospital to be checked for asthma. After talking to Troy for a short while I noticed a link between the times that he was getting chest infections and his fights. Basically, Troy would get a chest infection a few days before a fight and just before the start of the boxing season. I knew from my own experience that fear can come out in different ways in different people. My own fear or nerves had often shown up physically as a chesty cough and it was my prognosis that Troy's bad chests and supposed asthma were being caused by his own fears. I put this theory to Troy but he was far from convinced; however, he did agree to see me again the following week.

At the beginning of our next session Troy told me that he had had a very strange dream which didn't make sense to him. The very fact that he was mentioning it told me that it would be significant in one way or another. Troy said that he felt silly even telling me this but in his dream fluid was leaking from his brain and flowing down into his chest. When he told me this I nearly hit the ceiling. 'Troy, how much clearer do you want this message to be? Your subconscious mind is telling you that your chest infections are all coming from your head, it's so obvious.' I told him that his fears around fighting were manifesting themselves as a chest infection, which was his subconscious mind's way of protecting him, keeping him safe, and it was doing a great job; after all, how could he fight with a chest infection?

When Troy realised what he was doing he changed his focus and became much more positive. His chest infections disappeared, he didn't have asthma and he went on to win his next ten fights and become the amateur boxing association's novice title winner. He is now a professional boxer with several wins under his belt and ironically is being promoted by the legendary Barry McGuigan.

What Troy was doing here is what so many of us do in different ways all of the time. We know what we want to achieve but because that can be very scary we come up with ways of sabotaging ourselves, just like in this example, where Troy's subconscious mind created chest infections in an attempt to protect him from facing his fear. I have met people who have created all sorts of excuses as to why they can't go on towards their chosen goal. One guy who was about to take a giant step forward in his life convinced himself he had cancer, another had a nervous breakdown, another turned to drink. These all spring from fear; fear of change, fear of success, fear of failure, fear of not being good enough. The answer to these fears is to face them, dissect them and realise that the vast majority of them are illusions created by our own minds in a misguided attempt to keep us safe. It is often easier to stick with what we know, even though this might not be very good, rather than risk going into unknown territory. A good tip when faced with one of these fears is to ask yourself what's the worst that can happen? And then what? And then what? Keep going until you come up with an answer and then decide if you can deal with that answer.

After my sessions with Troy word got around and I started to work with lots more sportsmen including boxers, rugby players and speedway riders. Most of them introduced me as their sports psychologist; I guess in their eyes sports psychologist sounded better than counsellor. To be honest, I didn't care what they called me as long as we were getting results. I worked with Steve Bendall, a professional middleweight boxer who had lost his passion for the sport and was on a losing streak but who still wanted to win a title. After three fights Steve won the English middleweight title against a red-hot prospect who had won all twenty-three of his professional fights. Most people thought that Steve would be just another stepping stone on his way to the top but we had other ideas and Steve won the fight after ten gruelling rounds because he believed that he could.

I believe that my success in this area, as in many other areas, was due to the fact that I believed in what I was saying; I wasn't just talking the talk, as so many different types of coaches do, I could also walk the walk and that is unusual, as far as I can see. People can usually spot a genuine person. Even if it takes a little time to do so, the genuine man will come through in the end.

My friend Paul Browning was telling me how he was really excited to get the chance to meet the author of a great self-help book he had recently read. He met this lady at a network meeting and actually ended up sitting in her company, which he was over the moon about. He came away very disappointed and said that all this woman did was moan about how bad and hard her life was. It's very easy to write something or even say something but it's much harder to actually live by what you say and that's what makes the great people stand out.

My counselling work has taken me into many different areas such as depression, bereavement and many more. Recently, I have worked with people who have been suicidal and even the families of people who have committed suicide and I have found this the hardest area of all to work in.

In 2008 in the United Kingdom 5,706 people committed suicide.

To sit with parents whose child has committed suicide and to share just a fraction of their overwhelming pain is a real test of one's character and one I am not ashamed to say has touched me deeply. In fact, at times all I could do was to sit and cry with them.

I was asked by a local hospital if I would work with the families of people who had committed suicide or may have committed suicide. Quite often in these cases an open verdict is recorded by the coroner as evidence can be inconclusive and the only person who knows what happened for certain is no longer here. From a counselling point of view I knew this would be tough but also once again it would help me to grow as a counsellor so I accepted the offer without much hesitation.

It was to be some time before I worked with my first clients for the hospital. In the meantime, I had booked an appointment with a medium to get a reading as I was in turmoil about whether I had made the right decision to leave the fire service as financially things were still very tight. I guess I wanted some reassurance from a source that I had never really used but had always fascinated me. The world of mediums was one I had always wondered about and admired from a distance.

This lady, who was recommended by a friend, lived in Solihull, which was about 15 miles from my house.

While I was driving to her house for the appointment and at the same time wondering why I was doing such a stupid thing, my phone rang. As I was driving I didn't answer it until I was outside this lady's house. I listened to the voice message that had been left. It was the Hospital, telling me that they had a client for me to work with; it was the family of a young woman who had jumped from the top of a block of 16 story flats.

My heart sank. I had worked with individuals before but not families or even couples. My first reaction was to tell them thanks but no thanks. I decided that I would have to think about it later as I was about to see this medium.

The medium was a lovely lady who made me feel at home almost straight away. The first thing she said to me was, 'I am getting a young lady standing in front of me and I am also seeing a tall building that looks like a block of flats. She is beckoning you forward and saying work with the family. Does this make sense?'

I don't know what my face looked like but my thoughts were, how the fuck did she know that? I was totally amazed and to this day I don't know how that lady came up with the information that she did.

Suffice to say, I worked with the parents of the young lady and it was the hardest, most emotional work I have ever done in my counselling experience. They were such lovely people who were totally devastated at the loss of their precious child. Throughout their pain and grief they had dignity and always thought of other people going through similar events. They completely amazed me and I feel very honoured to have met them but I only wish it could have been in different circumstances. I also wish I could have met their daughter; she sounded like one of life's real characters. As they put it, a shining light had gone out of their lives. They were beautiful people who I will never forget. I did tell them about my experience with the medium and it did seem to give them some comfort, as did the counselling, but I have to say their grief was overwhelming and just so heartbreaking.

Suicide is a very complex area and one in which I certainly do not consider myself to be an expert by any stretch of the imagination. In the cases that I have worked on so far rejection certainly seems to have played a big part. But alcohol and the economic downturn also come into the equation. Interestingly, three times as many men as women kill themselves.

I think a lot of this comes down to men's role in society. They are told – or if not told then it is certainly implied in hundreds of different ways – that they should be tough, reliable, dependable and strong, to name but a few of the attributes to which all men are supposed to aspire. Speaking as a man I don't always feel strong, dependable, tough or logical. Sometimes I get scared, sometimes I feel weak, vulnerable and sad and I feel as though I am failing; sometimes I need support.

The problems seem to occur when things go wrong – I lose my job, my partner leaves me, maybe for another man. My mask of being this tough macho man slips, my vulnerability shows. 'Shit, what will everyone think of me? They will see that underneath this macho mask I am just a frightened little boy. I feel rejected. How could they fire me after twenty years of loyal service? How could she leave me just like that? I want my job back. Who am I without a job? How can I provide for my family? I am the man, the breadwinner, or at least I should be. I want my wife back. Who am I without a partner? Who else will love me or even want me? I can't even hang on to my job, my wife – what type of a man am I? Am I a real man?'

Not only do we feel rejected by society or our loved ones but we start to question who we really are and then worst of all we reject ourselves. It can seem at this point as if our world closes down, that the only way out is to end it all, it is the final throw of the dice. I eventually get to take some power back by making the biggest decision of all – to end my own life. You may have rejected me but now I will reject you in one final violent move. When somebody feels like this it must feel as though they have no control over their own life but this final act allows them to take back the control, and in a big way. When people are depressed their worlds tend to get smaller and smaller; they hide away, stay at home, avoid people; they don't see possibilities, only negativity. The answer here is to open up their worlds again, show them that they have options, show them that people do care.

Once again they have made the illusion real, only this time it is a very dark and depressing illusion with seemingly no way out. I have felt very low myself at different times in my life. Even though I know these feelings and what I am creating are just illusions, when I am in them they feel and appear very real. It can be very hard to step back, detach and look at the picture from a different viewpoint. Quite often it is when we do this that we see the illusion for what it really is; just a bundle of thoughts that we have created in the sanctuary of our own minds.

I have worked with women who have been raped, including gang raped. I have worked with men and women who have been sexually abused. These are tough areas to work in and I sometimes feel a sense of despair when I hear how some human beings can treat other human beings.

Most of the people I see are suffering from depression or have just lost their way in life. Some people get very upset, some people get very angry. I have had clients say that they want to sleep with me, which strokes my ego but is usually a sign of someone who needs to sexualise their relationships as a way of taking control. After all, sex can be a very powerful tool. I have only ever met one client with whom I struggled to get along. He was a salesman who would brag about sacking his staff and making them cry. He only came to see me because his wife insisted after his latest affair that he get counselling or face a divorce. So he went through the motions of seeing me to appease her but he made it clear that he did not want or need help.

The guy was in serious need of help but people who go to see a coach or counsellor reluctantly (usually to please others) are very hard work. Change requires the person really to want to change and part of this process is actually asking for help.

If you are feeling low or desperate please ask for help; it will come in one form or another.

Most major religions talk about a fear of separation. In Christianity, Adam and Eve are separated from God by being thrown from the Garden of Eden (heaven). Ever since that time, according to religion man has strived to reconnect with God and become whole again. A baby is separated from its mother at birth and its umbilical cord is cut but the baby's natural survival instincts tell it to reconnect with its mother straight away. When a relationship ends people will often say that they feel as though a part of them is missing.

In his great book, *The Gift of Fear*, Gavin de Becker says that public speaking is one of the biggest fears in the world. His theory is that if we stand up to talk and the group rejects us then this taps in to an innate feeling that goes all the way back to our caveman days when to be excluded by the tribe would almost certainly mean death. Logically, you know that if the audience reject you it doesn't mean that you are going to die; however, at this point we are talking about feelings and they are anything but logical. The feeling part of you believes that it is going to die and that is terrifying and that is why most people won't even attempt to stand up and talk to a group of people because of the dreaded fear of rejection. What if I am not good enough? They will all laugh at me, I will feel stupid, I won't fit in and – at a deeper emotional level – I will die. If my wife or partner leaves me, what does that say about me? I am a crap partner, no one will want me, I can't be any good in bed, I couldn't keep her happy, and where do I fit into society? I am no longer a husband or a wife, what does that make me?

I really like this theory of separation and feel as though it is at the root of a lot of our problems, but is it true? What are we being separated from? An image that society and our upbringing have formed for us – but is that real? It has been created, so the good news is that we can recreate it in a different way. Will I die if the crowd reject me? I know this is a powerful feeling but if we delve into it, is it true? I am not a religious man by any stretch of the imagination but I do believe in God; however, my God loves me. He put me on this earth and he wants me to experience life to the full – is he likely to reject me? I don't think so!! What would God have to gain by rejecting me?

The only person who can reject you is you, so how can we stop these old patterns of rejection from happening? First of all we need to bring them into our awareness – what are these feelings of rejection or separation? We need to look at them and dissect them, pull them apart. The worst thing we can do is to ignore them; in doing this they just get bigger and bigger until they are so big that it is virtually impossible to ignore them any longer. What you resist will persist, what you think about will become real and grow. Dive into the feelings. From my own experience, whenever I have faced my fears I have found them to be seriously lacking in any substance. I am talking about the fear we create, not the fear that keeps us safe. If, for example, I see a tiger running towards me I want my real fear to kick in and give me a massive burst of adrenalin that will make me run like the wind.

What you resist will persist. What you focus on you will get, so if you focus on being alone, scared, weak then that's what you will get; however, by the same token, if you focus on being happy, strong, lovable then that is what you will get.

Be very careful with your influences. We are being constantly bombarded with negativity; bad news sells. I personally don't buy a tabloid newspaper or watch soaps. We can't help meeting negative people on a daily basis but we don't have to invite them around for tea. Don't get drawn into negativity. Yes, those types of people will be negative about you and may even reject you but think about it, what have you lost? And more importantly, what have you gained?

Be very careful with your self-talk. We are constantly talking ourselves in and out of things. What we say to ourselves is vital. Four centuries ago Pascal wrote, 'Man is so made that by continually telling him he is a fool, he believes it, and by continually telling it to himself he makes himself believe it. For man holds an inward talk with self alone, which it behoves [sic] him to regulate well.'

Words are like seeds; they are very powerful. Be careful what you say to others, your words will have an effect, and be very careful in what you say to yourself. Choose what seeds you want to plant. I like love seeds and inspirational seeds.

The way you think will have a massive effect on your life; for example, if your thoughts are negative then your life will surely be negative. It follows that if your thoughts are positive then your life will be positive. You will see great opportunities and be surrounded with like-minded people. I believe that our thoughts create our world; your thoughts can make you ill or heal you. Your thoughts can make you feel happy or sad. You are the world; you are the centre of the world, think about this. If something happens to you and you die then the world ends; at least, your world ends on this plane. This is why things like self-affirmations work – they are a way of conditioning your thoughts and whatever you think about on a constant basis is what you will become.

People just don't practise this. I explain this process to boxers, for example, and then they go away feeling very positive for a while. They usually come back to see me if or when they lose a fight. The first thing I say to them is have you been working on your positive affirmations and visualisations? I already know what they are going to say and it is always, without fail, 'No, I haven't, Tony.'

These things need to be practised every day. It is no secret that to be good at anything takes practice and this applies even more so with controlling something as powerful as the way we think, which in turn will control the way we live our lives.

What have you got to lose by continuously talking positively to yourself? This may not come easily – after all, we are trying to undo years of negativity – but persevere, you will like the results.

I believe we have been fed this myth of separation from God but what if we are all God? Then how can we be separate from ourselves? We have been told that to get back to God we must do this or that but what if we are already there and God is within us and indeed has never left? What if the important question was not 'What if I am not good enough?' but 'What if I am good enough already, just as I am?'? I dare you to take a positive attitude, place God at your side and explore this question. Say to yourself with feeling, 'I AM ACTUALLY OK! I AM MAGNIFICENT!!

Because you are! All of your future decisions will then come from a place of being magnificent instead of a place of not being good enough. How can your world not change with this totally new perspective?

OUTCOMES

What have I learned? Firstly, most of the old clichés we hear so often are true. We must learn to love ourselves before we can believe that other people can love us. If you don't even like you, then why would anyone else like you? Why would anyone want to be in your company when even you don't like your own company? What are your good points? What are your achievements so far in this life? I have found that when I aim high, even if I miss I still end up higher than if I had aimed low.

The vast majority of people are living an act, too scared to be themselves, whoever or whatever that may be. We feel that we have to act a certain way to survive in today's society. Men act tough, macho, they don't do feelings; they feel them, they know they are there but they don't show or even talk about them. Men have been given an image to live up to; the action man doll represents that image, scar, muscles and all. But dolls don't have emotions, they don't do feelings. You can throw them around, leave them in the corner for hours or days, then pick them up again and play with them as if nothing has ever happened and even bend or mould them back into their original shape.

Women have to be pretty to compete with each other, to match the images in glossy magazines. Barbie doll represents the image they have to live with and compete with. Some of these dolls do cry but they are crocodile tears that can be refilled with tap water. They are not real, deep, from-the-heart tears.

Society has laid down these blueprints of how real men and women should look and behave but in reality this is impossible. However, when we feel that we don't live up to these goals or impossible targets we start to feel inadequate, useless, a failure.

You can rewrite your script; that's right, I did say write your own script because at the moment you are living your life according to other people's scripts and the labels that you have been given. Then you wonder why you are not happy, why you feel unfulfilled, because it's not your script, it's society's script, the tabloid newspapers' script, the glossy magazines' script. According to their scripts you can never be good enough, no matter what you do.

It is my experience that everyone is searching for something – the meaning of life, why are we here? Who am I?

What stops us from achieving those great things that we know deep down inside that we are more than capable of achieving? Why are we even scared to try to reach our goals? Why do we play and stay safe? People are looking for easy answers and even more people are queuing up to provide those easy answers at a price, of course, and why not?

It's my belief that you already have the answers; yes, of course we all need guidance, a helping hand at times, but deep down you know what you have to do.

What if God played a trick on the human race? We are all searching for answers; we search high and low, far and wide. Man has travelled to every corner of the globe and even beyond the globe and into outer space.

But what if God knew that this would happen? What if he could predict our futures? After all, he is God. He would have known that we would climb every mountain and journey to the depths of the sea and fly out into space. In our search for answers, in our search for God, he has hidden in the one place we would never think to look; he is right under our noses (literally). We are all looking out when in truth we only need to look within. The one place that the majority of the human race has never looked is deep within their own souls, God's secret hiding place. So what is God? God is love. Learn to love yourself, and truly love yourself, and then you can start to love others.

There are no easy answers, no magic wands, and no tablets to take. The journey is the answer; stay on the path. Is it easy? No, of course it's not! Can it be done? Most definitely, you are doing it anyway. By facing your fears you can change your perception and change your so-called fears into opportunities. We learn through experience, so why not go out and experience as much as you can?

Once you have experienced something your mind will expand and it will never shrink back to what it previously was; it can't, those new experiences will be stored in your subconscious mind, to be called upon whenever they are needed. Experiences can be scary but they are also exciting and that is what is missing from most people's lives. The opposite of excitement is boredom and I don't know about you but I would rather have a life full of excitement than boredom. Facing your fears is definitely exciting; make your goals exciting, make your relationships exciting.

My own biggest fear is that one day I will look back over my life and feel as though I have wasted it. To me the biggest crime known to man is that of wasting a life, wasting this golden and exciting opportunity that we have all been given.

I have learned to stop blaming everyone else and stop blaming my circumstances, take responsibility and create the life that I want to live and not live the life that someone else, no matter how well intentioned, has created for me.

It is my experience that people are often very reluctant to take responsibility for their own actions. While I am blaming you for the things that have gone wrong in my life, I will not have to change. What's even more relevant is that, while I blame you and leave all future decisions to you, I can carry on blaming you when things go wrong. It's never my fault. This is usually because people doubt their ability to make decisions, and they are scared of making mistakes because this will just confirm the low opinion that they have of themselves. We need to step up to the mark and take responsibility for our own actions. That doesn't mean I am responsible for everybody else's actions but I am certainly responsible for my own. This is the first step towards lasting change.

I have always felt from the time I was a small child that I have been guided. Being raised as a

Catholic, my mum used to say that we all had a guardian angel watching over us. Now, I don't pretend to know about angels or spirits or even God, but I do know that this belief that I am being guided has been a big comfort to me when times were hard. To be able to call on this mysterious guardian angel or spirit has helped me to step in to the unknown many times. It is also my belief that if I am guided then so are you; the phrase 'ask and you will receive' comes to mind.

So ask! What have you got to lose?

You have been given a great gift; don't waste it. Go forward in peace, love and excitement to serve others. I will let you in on a secret – it is when I have been serving others that all of my own needs have been met.

Remember to forgive yourself; you are a human being. You are not superman or superwoman. It's OK to be scared, jealous, happy, sad. Stop beating yourself up, you are perfect just as you are. Remember to love yourself. You are beautiful. Take the time and say these words now, with real feeling and really mean it, don't just go through the motions, say it out loud, several times: I AM MAGNIFICENT!! Because you are, and now is the time to shine.

I will end with this short poem that I have called 'Remember Who You Really Are!'. I believe it is when we forget who we really are that we get scared and full of self-doubts.

Remember Who You Really Are!

Wake up!!! Time is slipping by, move it! Come on, get going, it's time to wake from your slumber. Dust off your swords, pick up your armour; the enemy is much closer than you think.

While you slumbered he has climbed through the walls of your mind. He has softened your body, your mind and your spirit. Decay has silently entered your bloodstream and is spreading like the darkness spreads through the night.

The alarm is sounding, its shrill is piercing, and it is late, but not too late. The kingdom of God is within but so is the enemy. There is a battle to be fought, no time to plan. Call on your inner strengths: integrity, honesty, faith, self-acceptance and trust. Remember who you are and why you are here.

The fertile soil of your mind is being poisoned as we speak. Turn in when you want to turn away, fight when every single part of you wants to run.

Once again, just like a thousand times before, the easy path has become hard. Now it's time to take the hard path that you have avoided like the plague.

FIGHTER, RESCUER, HEALER

Remember who you really are!

When you get scared, when fear holds you in its vice-like grip, remember who you are!

Centuries of battle have hardened you; your ancestors are rising for battle once more. Jesus, Buddha, Ghandi are all coursing through your veins; you cannot lose, have faith.

Let the light shine through the darkness, illuminate the universe with your love, and remember who you really are!

To find out more about Tony please go to:
www.tonysomers.com